AF305026

witchology

witchology

an illustrated compendium of magical know-how

Cerridwen Greenleaf

CICO BOOKS

To the wise women in my family; I learn from you still.

Published in 2026 by CICO Books
An imprint of Ryland Peters & Small Ltd
20–21 Jockey's Fields
London WC1R 4BW
www.rylandpeters.com
Email: euregulations@rylandpeters.com

10 9 8 7 6 5 4 3 2 1

Text in this book has previously appeared in *The Book of Kitchen Witchery, 5-Minute Magic for Modern Wiccans, The Magical Home, The Book of Witchy Wellbeing, Your Book of Shadows,* and *Spells for Peace of Mind.*

A CIP record for this book is available from the British Library.
US Library of Congress CIP data has been applied for.

ISBN: 978-1-80065-587-4

Printed in China

Commissioning editor: Kristine Pidkameny
Desk editor: Imogen Valler-Miles
Senior designer: Emily Breen
Art director: Sally Powell
Creative director: Leslie Harrington
Production manager: Gordana Simakovic
Publishing manager: Carmel Edmonds

The authorised representative in the EEA is
Authorised Rep Compliance Ltd.,
Ground Floor. 71 Lower Baggot Street,
Dublin, D01 P593, Ireland
www.arccompliance.com

SAFETY NOTE

Neither the author nor the publisher can be held responsible for any claim arising out of the general information and practices provided in this book. While the use of essential oils, herbs, incense, and particular practices refer to healing benefits, they are not intended to replace diagnosis of illness or ailments, or healing or medicine. Always consult your doctor or other health professional in the case of illness. Essential oils are very powerful and potentially toxic if used too liberally. Follow the advice given on the label and never use the oils neat on bare skin, or if pregnant without consulting a health professional. The safe and proper use of candles and incense is the sole responsibility of the person using them. Never burn a candle or incense on or near anything that might catch fire and do not leave unattended. Keep out of the reach of children and pets and ensure good ventilation.

contents

introduction

Welcome to the wonderful world of Wicca. Commonly called witchcraft, or the craft, Wicca is an ancient spiritual pagan practice that is centered in earth wisdom. In its essence, Wicca is intended to aid our evolution, both individually and communally. It helps us maintain spiritual harmony with the earth and the stars, while also balancing our relationships with others. Witchcraft reflects the very soul of humanity, celebrating the richness of the natural world and the beauty of the human heart. People often think of witchcraft as a solitary undertaking, but it was originally nurtured and informed by groups of friends passing on herbal remedies, exchanging favorite plant seeds, and working rituals together in covens. On the wings of alliance, witchcraft flew and grew to be practiced worldwide.

Magical moments are very important; they signify that we have stepped out of the routine of the ordinary day-to-day and are exploring a higher consciousness. Magic and spellwork are about expansion—expanding your horizons, enriching your mind and spirit, and celebrating the real riches of well-being and contentment. While many of the sabbat celebrations featured in this book are group gatherings, much of your spellcraft will be performed by a coven of one—you. And it is the "inner work" of devising and creating personal rituals that will encourage your deepest spiritual development.

Magic resides inside of us; we create it with our thoughts and actions. It is our deepest power and we are born with it. I began practicing the craft as a child. For me, witchcraft was and is the most natural thing in the world—and indeed it is all about being in the natural world. On woodland walks, my Aunt Edith pointed out nettles, wild mint, Queen Anne's lace, and other herbs that grew by the creek beds near my home. We picked, steeped, and sipped concoctions we made together as she imparted her homely wisdom. Little did I know at the time I was being gently schooled as an apprentice kitchen witch.

There are many strands to witchcraft, and kitchen witchery is just one of them. Others include green witchery or hedge witchery, and you need not feel limited to just one path—indeed, I encompass elements from each in my personal practice. All have, at their core, a respect for and connection to nature and the earth.

Within the pages of this book, you will discover everything you need to know to get started on your path to a magical life. You will be guided through the witch's tool kit and the basics of spellwork before exploring other magical items—such as teas, herbs, essential oils, and crystals—to incorporate into your practice. You will then discover how you can harness the energies of the moon and perform your spells at the optimal time in the lunar cycle to maximize your power. Finally, you will learn about the festivals and ceremonies that mark the witchy calendar, with suggestions for how you can celebrate these seasonal holidays.

I hope that this book will encourage and empower you to find and embrace your own personal magic!

CHAPTER ONE

tools of the trade: from altars to wands

Discover the witch's tool kit for your wielding of the craft. Your tools collect and hold the magic that lives inside of you. If you treat them with the utmost respect, your tools will serve you very well—they will become a source of power for you and magnify the strength of your ritual work.

the altar

An altar is a physical point of focus for your rituals. It is your sacred workspace—a place imbued with your personal pagan power—and is key to your magical workings. This space will doubtless become a touchstone for you where you immediately step into the realm of magic.

Your altar should contain a collection of beloved objects that are assembled in a meaningful manner. These can include crystals, candles, incense, flowers, sculptures, and so on—anything that appeals to you symbolically. Here is where you can fully apply your personal design and creativity. Tap into your intuition and let it be your guide.

Altars can be created in different places and for different purposes—we'll explore a few ideas over the following pages. An altar can be anything from a rock in the forest to an exquisitely carved antique table. Even portable or temporary altars can suffice, such as a board suspended between two chairs for "rituals on the go."

Whatever you use for your altar, it will represent the four directions of the compass. I recommend setting up an altar to face north, long believed to be the origin of primordial energy. North is also the direction of the midnight hour, sometimes known as the "witching hour," and an altar oriented in this fashion promises potent magic. To be fully imbued with energy, your magical tools should reside on your altar.

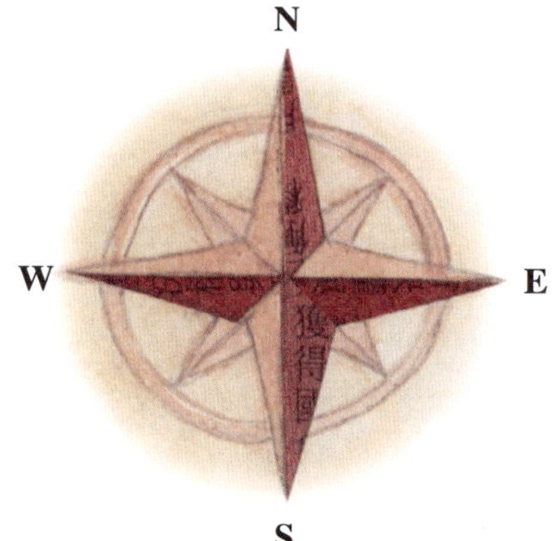

a wellness altar

Creating a wellness altar will safeguard your physical health and that of your loved ones. First, drape a piece of white fabric over your altar for clean and clear new beginnings. Next, take two green candles, place them in green glass holders, and position them in the two farthest corners. Then place your censer (see page 22) exactly in the middle and burn camphor, sandalwood, or frankincense for purification.

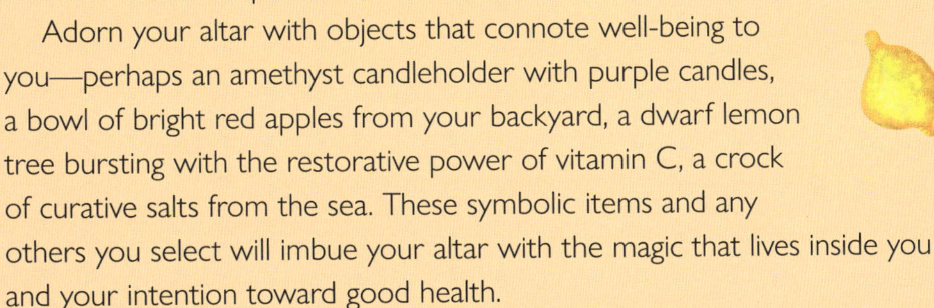

Adorn your altar with objects that connote well-being to you—perhaps an amethyst candleholder with purple candles, a bowl of bright red apples from your backyard, a dwarf lemon tree bursting with the restorative power of vitamin C, a crock of curative salts from the sea. These symbolic items and any others you select will imbue your altar with the magic that lives inside you and your intention toward good health.

It is imperative that your altar be pleasing to your eye and fill you with gladness when you gaze upon it. After you have been performing midnight-hour rituals there for a while, a positive healing energy field will radiate from your altar.

a kitchen altar

The kitchen is the perfect place to create an altar since it is considered the heart of the home. On a low table or chest, place a forest-green cloth and a brown candle to represent family and home. Add lovely objects you have gathered, including items from your garden and the outdoors—ocean-carved driftwood, a gorgeous flower, a dried seedpod, a favorite crystal, for example.

It is of the utmost importance to add a bouquet of wildflowers native to your area, which you should have gathered or bought locally. This posy will help integrate you and your home into your neighborhood and geographic region. Also add a sweetly scented sachet of herbs such as mint, rosemary, lavender, or thyme to imbue your space with positive energy—see page 70 for more ideas.

Burn essential oils in an oil lamp, choosing those which will create an aura of comfort around your kitchen, such as vanilla, cinnamon, or sweet-orange neroli. (For other ideas, see pages 78–79.) Finally, anoint the brown candle with an essential oil, concentrating on the power of peace and bliss surrounding your home and all around your kitchen altar.

Chant the words below:

Peace and plenty are in abundance,
And here true bliss surrounds.
From now on, all disharmony is gone,
This is a place of powerful blessings,
For here lives sheer joy.
And so it is—blessed be!

This consecrated space connects you to the earth of which you are a part and will ease your spirits at any time.

seasonal altars

Your altar helps you to maintain balance in your life and deepen your spiritual connection to the world around you. A seasonal altar is your tool for ceremonies to honor Mother Nature and receive the deep wisdom of the earth by blending the energies of shells, feathers, leaves, flowers, herbs, and all of the gifts of the season. Opposite are some ideas for seasonal altar decorations.

Alternatively, you could switch your altar adornments every two or three days with the changing of the lunar cycles (see Chapter 5) and also to mark the sabbats (see pages 118–119).

spring

You can create a wonderful outdoor altar for spring by planning two seasons ahead and planting floral bulbs—flowers that are the very harbingers of spring such as tulips and lilies of the valley. When the bulbs begin to grow and bud, place an image or statue in the center of your altar, which could be a stone bench or the top of a rock wall. It could be a bust of a mythological youth to represent Hyacinth, immortalized in myth and in the gorgeous flower itself. Throughout the spring, you can stand inside your magic circle (see page 41) and pray and chant for the rebirth of nature that is spring.

summer

During the season of sun and heat, the fullness of life and growth can be celebrated with the colors of yellow, green, and red. As you go on vacation, bring back shells and stones and create an altar devoted to this season of joy. I have an outdoor fireplace, which is my seasonal shrine, and I adorn it with a lei of orchids, a spell bottle filled with sparkly golden sand, and gleaming shells from the beach. A yellow votive candle placed in a gorgeous opalescent abalone shell gently flames. An old brick imprinted with an image of the sun sits upright, standing guard over the humble shrine to the season of Helios, the Greek god of the sun.

fall

Bring the bounty of the harvest to your kitchen altar. The leaves are falling and reaping-time is here. Now is the time for a gratitude altar reflecting the abundance and continuity of life. An arrangement of pumpkins, acorns, multicolored branches, and a handsome wreath will honor this time of abundance.

winter

White and blue represent snow and sky. Star-shaped candles and a bare branch on your altar symbolize this time to go within, explore the inner reaches of self, and draw forth the insight for the coming spring. If you have a fireplace inside, this can be your altar for the coldest season, with candles burning to help create comfort and warmth.

the cauldron

Representing the Goddess (see page 131), the round basin of the cauldron is symbolic of the womb from which we all came. Ideally made of cast iron or another durable metal that heats uniformly, the cauldron can hold fire and represents rebirth—the phoenix rising from the ashes of the past. Usually, cauldrons stand on three legs for practicality, stability, and mobility. You can place one on your altar if there is room or on the floor to the left of the altar with all other representations of the energy of the female and the Goddess.

In spring, this sacred basin can be used to hold earth or water and, in the winter season, it should hold fire—candle flames or sweet-smoked incense, which signifies the rebirth of the sun to come at the end of the coldest season. You can also be playful with the form the cauldron takes and use a rain-filled urn or a flower-filled fountain. Summer's cauldron can be a beautiful cup; at harvest-time, use a pumpkin or another hollowed-out gourd. You can play with the vessel concept in your own ceremonies and be imaginative—get really creative.

A classic cast-iron cauldron is very useful for mixing herbs and essential oils (see Chapter 3)—just make sure to clean it thoroughly after each use so as not to mix energies inadvertently. You can scry with a cauldron full of water to foresee the future by reading images on the surface of the water, as well as use this magical vessel for burning papers upon which you have written spells, incantations, and magical intentions. In doing this, you are sending your wishes to the gods and goddesses through the flames, the element of fire.

the chalice

Another vessel symbolizing the feminine, the Goddess, and fertility, the chalice is a goblet dedicated specially for use on your altar. Holding both physical fluid and waters of our emotional body, it is connected to the element of water. Place your carefully chosen chalice on the left side of your altar. A grail is also a chalice. Legend tells that the Holy Grail brought life back to the decaying kingdom of Camelot and restored King Arthur and his people to health, giving rise to the rebirth of England itself.

On your altar, your chalice can hold water, mead, wine, juice, or anything that has been blessed. It can contain holy water for consecrations and blessing rites. At the end of many ritual ceremonies and sabbats, it is customary to toast the deities with a hearty ale, cider, or wine and thank them for being present. After the magic circle has been opened (see page 41), you can pour the contents of your chalice into the ground outdoors as an offering to benevolent entities.

the broom

Also called a besom, this magical tool was born centuries ago from the practical magic of sweeping the ritual area clean before casting a spell. With focus and intention, you can dispel negative energy and bad spirits from the area and prepare a space for ritual work (see pages 33–36 to find out more). In bygone days, pagan marriages took place with a leap over the broom. Over the centuries, this rich history began to capture the imagination as the archetypal symbol of witches.

Your broom is an essential tool for energy management. You don't have to wait until you are performing spellcraft to use it—you can purify after a squabble with a loved one, to rid yourself of a bout of the blues, or any upset you need to sweep out of your home. Many a kitchen witch begins the day with this simple ritual of a clean sweep to freshen surroundings and to make room for good energy.

broom etiquette

This is very important—do not use your ritual broom for housecleaning. The use of your magical broom is not intended to make your house spotless; rather, it is a symbolic act that is effective in maintaining your home as a personal sanctuary. Like me, you may well view every inch of your home as sacred space, but you will need to keep your regular housekeeping implements separate from those you use for your magical workings. Think of it as a separation of church and state, if you will. It pretty much is!

The Wiccan tradition holds brooms in high regard, and some witches have an impressive collection of brooms, each one named to distinguish their roles as "familiars," or kindred spirits. Kitchen witches often have the most extensive bevy of brooms of anyone.

sourcing your purification broom

You can obtain a handmade broom from a craft fair or your favorite metaphysical five-and-dime. This should not be a machine-made plastic one from the supermarket, although I did get a long cinnamon-infused rush broom from Trader Joe's that I use in my witch's kitchen. A broom made of wood and woven of natural straw will be imbued with the inherent energies of those organic materials.

To purify your space with as much of your own personal energy as possible, a broom you have crafted by hand is best. You can make your own purification broom from straw bound together and attached to a fallen tree branch, or you can add some mojo to a store-bought broom.

Wrap copper wire around the bottom of your broom handle and also use it to bind straw to a sturdy stick or branch for the DIY kind. Venus-ruled copper lends an aura of beauty and keeps negativity at bay. Attach crystals to the handle with glue to boost your broom's power. Recommended crystals for space clearing and purification are as follows:

- **Amber** for good cheer.
- **Blue lace agate** for tranquility and a peaceful home.
- **Coral** for well-being.
- **Jet** absorbs bad energy.
- **Onyx** is a stone of protection.
- **Petrified wood** for security.
- **Tiger's eye** will protect you from energy-draining situations or people.
- **Turquoise** creates calm and relaxation.

AMBER

JET

TURQUOISE

spell bottles

Also called magic bottles, spell bottles have been around since the 1600s and were often filled with hair, nails, blood, and other kind of ephemera. Now, they are used to empower us and adorn our sacred spaces.

Though their popularity has waned since the Elizabethan age when they were called "witch bottles," spell bottles are still used for a variety of intentions. You can customize your own spell-in-a-bottle with crystal stoppers and you should let your imagination run wild as to the usage and positive purposes with which you can fill your vessels—for example, you could put one in your garden to keep your plants healthy, one in the bedroom to bring love and happiness, and a spell bottle on the living room mantel to protect your home.

Spell bottles are primarily used for protection, but you can also put symbols of your dreams and desires in them, such as cinnamon for the spice of life, a rose for romance, and rosemary for remembrance.

ritual knives

The knives you use to slice bread and chop veggies are in a completely different category from these special knives.

the athame

Pronounced "a-tha-may," this is your magical knife, or it can also be a ritual dagger or sword. The athame represents and contains yang energy, the male aspect of the deities, and it is also associated with the element of fire. For these two reasons, your athame should be placed on the right side of your altar. It is to be used to direct the energies raised in your circles and spellwork; because it is not used for cutting but rather for the manipulation of the forces involved in the work of enchantment, an athame is usually a dull blade. Some Wiccan traditionalists specify that the handle should be black or very dark in color, since black is the color that absorbs energies and, therefore, becomes quickly attuned to the practitioner.

the bolline

A bolline, pronounced "bowl-in," is most often a white-handled knife with a curved blade. It is used for making other tools and for cutting materials such as cords and herbs. You can create your own wand, for example, with the help of your bolline (see page 24). This increases the energy held within the wand and creates a magical tool by using a magical tool. You can also use your bolline to carve symbols and names into your candles, wands, and other tools. Like the athame, the bolline is also associated with male energy.

censers and incense

A censer, pronounced "sen-ser" and also known as a thurible, is an incense burner and represents the elements of air and fire. Nowadays, there is an incredible variety of censers available, so follow your instincts as to what is best for you. Place your censer at the very center of your altar.

Incense is a way to bless your space and also to purify your tools, your mind, and your space with the sacred smoke in preparation for spellwork. The evocative scent and soft, billowing smoke will transport you in a sensory way. Incense contains inherent energies that you can use to augment your intention and further power your magical purpose. I have learned much about different kinds of incense—loose, cone, stock, and cylinder—as well as the best kinds of herbs to use from experimentation, asking elders, and observing magi at work.

It is a good idea to test your incense before using it in ritual, especially before organizing a group circle, to see how much smoke is produced to avoid any problems; and it's best to check with your fellow participants to make sure no one has any respiratory problems or sensitivities. If you can't burn incense for any such reason, you can use another air symbol instead, such as feathers, potpourri, fresh flowers, or even a paper fan.

candles

Candles are used by folk from all walks of life for relaxation, meditation, aromatherapy, and to achieve that "peaceful homey" feeling of being in your own sanctuary. This simple yet profound tool can make powerful magic. Take a moment to notice how candlelight transforms a dark room and fills the atmosphere with the energy of magical light. Every candle contains all four of the elemental energies:

- Earth: The solid wax forms the candle.
- Air: Oxygen feeds and fans the candle flame.
- Fire: The flame sparks and blazes.
- Water: Melted wax is the fluid elemental state.

I recommend keeping an array of sizes, shapes, and colors on hand. See pages 42–45 for more information about working with candles.

the wand

A magical wand is a powerful tool. Like an athame, a wand focuses, projects, and directs energy. Because it gathers and stores magical power, a wand is wonderful for healing and can be the device with which you draw the shape when you cast the circle (see page 41).

You can purchase a wand—just be sure to purify it, cleansing the energy of the shop so it is truly yours. However, if possible, try to find your wand in a serendipitous manner, drawing it to you through attraction. Take a walk in a nearby park or the woods. You may very well find the wand of your dreams in the form of a fallen tree branch. If you live near the ocean, you might find the perfect weathered wand on a beach as driftwood. Never cut a wand straight from a tree as the energy from harming the tree will be retained by the wand. Allow Mother Nature to choose one for you; she is always right. The most important factor for any wand is how it feels in your hand. You will know immediately when you have found the right one.

When you have found your wand, use sand paper to sand it to smoothness. If it is too long, use your bolline to cut it down to 12 inches (30 cm), or your preferred length. Wrap copper wire around the top and affix a crystal to the end to use as the pointer. Your wand should look beautiful to your eye so embellish it with ornaments you love, such as gems, crystals, beads, sequins, seashells, or whatever pleases you and adds to the power of this sacred implement.

witchy wood

Remember that each tree has distinctive properties so you may wish to tailor your choice of wood to your magical intentions.

- **Ash** grows fast and its seedlings root everywhere, so it's persistent. I recommend an ash wand for prosperity and self-improvement spells.
- **Birch** has feminine energy and healing power. Use a birch wand for healing spells, calming situations, and requesting a diplomatic solution.
- **Crab apple** will provide bent, gnarled wands. The apple tree is the tree of knowledge and wisdom. Apples—the fruit and the wood—are extremely useful to witchcraft. Use an apple wand whenever you need guidance, want to know the truth, or simply as an everyday wand.
- **Linden** wands have powerful healing properties and the trees are connected to positivity and light, bright energy.
- **Oak** has a strong masculine energy and is good for healing and protection. It makes a long-lasting wand for intensely focused work. If you choose to use only one wand, make it oak.
- **Osage orange** uplifts and inspires. It will produce a healing wand that can also be used to call forth spirit guides and animal guardians.
- **Rowan or mountain ash** is a "portal tree"—when you want to undertake a journey or a guided visualization, keep your rowan or mountain ash wand close by.

essential oils

These are natural oils made by distillations of herbs and flowers, ideally organic. They retain the fragrance of the original plant from which they are made. If you are making a potion or lotion to apply to the skin, it is important to mix essential oils with a carrier (or base) oil—such as jojoba, almond, apricot kernel, grape-seed, or sesame—to dilute the essential oil for safe skin application. Always test a blend on a small area of the skin first and leave for 24 hours to check you don't have any reaction to it. Find out more about essential oils and carrier oils on pages 74–79.

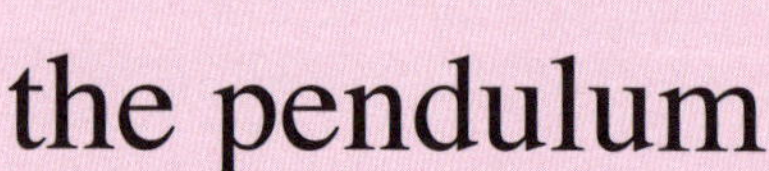

the pendulum

This witchy tool helps with decision making. Pendulums are easily bought at any metaphysical or New Age shop or mind, body, spirit bookstore, but you can also make your own. To do this, you'll need a 12-inch (30-cm) strip of string or leather cord and a small rose quartz with a pointy end.

Knot the quartz onto your cord and test it to show you which is "yes" and which is "no." This is done by asking it yes/no questions that you know the answer to, then observing its responses—you will notice it swings in a different way for each one, for example, round in a circle clockwise or counterclockwise, or back and forth.

your book of shadows

Here we have one of the most essential tools of all—a witch's recipe record, a ledger for all your magical workings, including spells, rituals, and results. This is your journal of all you have practiced and wrought as well as your research. Are your spells more effective during the new moon in the water signs of Cancer, Pisces, or Scorpio? That may well be unique to you and as you arrive at these important discoveries, you should write them down in your Book of Shadows so you know your true power as tested by time.

This is not just a ledger, though; it is a living document that you can apply to magical workings to come and will even help you design your own spells and ritual recipes. All the astrology, herb lore, crystal properties, lunar signs, and seasonal information will come into play as you experiment and uncover what works best for you. By keeping my own Book of Shadows, I was able to conclude that the new moon in Pisces is a super-powered time for my spells.

This is a book you will turn to again and again and your Book of Shadows should be very appealing to you. It can be a gorgeous, one-of-a-kind volume made with handmade paper and uniquely tooled bindings, or it can be a simple three-ring binder. Choose whatever is most useful to you.

CHAPTER TWO

spellwork basics: successful enchantments

Spells and rituals can arise from your needs, imagination, or the seasonal and traditional ceremonies that you find in this book and others. Understanding the basics of spellwork and being properly prepared will ensure you are equipped with everything you need to get the best results.

magical guidelines

Magic has rules. Known as the Wiccan Rede, the "bylaws" of Wicca were developed and shared in the 1970s. They provide an excellent guide of conduct for practicing witchcraft—not the "black magic" that led to witches being shunned, punished, and scourged, but magic with positive intentions for the greater good.

Although there are several bylaws, the Wiccan Rede can be summed up with one golden rule: "Do unto others as you would have others do unto you." In other words, the "right" action is up to you and is of paramount importance. With good intentions, you can learn to become a responsible ritualist. Always consider the short- or long-term effect of your rituals, and how yourself and others will be affected. Careful consideration will go a long way toward increasing the effectiveness of your work.

To craft beautiful, and more importantly, meaningful rituals to enrich your life, provide comfort, and maintain harmony and balance, I recommend following these three simple guidelines:

Trust your intuition.

Go with your instincts.

Listen to your heart.

preparing for spellwork

Call forth your powers within to make magic with ritual. Your mind and will are potent magical tools, and ritual is the practice of exercising your will.

First, identify your intention—see page 32. A well-defined intention is the key to success in any ritual. If your intention is not crystal clear, you are likely to fail. Approach your ritual concentrating fully on a definite aim.

With your intention set, plan and prepare for your ritual. Gather your ingredients and tools together. Part of your preparation should also include identifying and using correspondences—symbolic links between an item and your magical intention—to add to the depth and meaning of your ritual. These include candle color, the day of the week, as well as symbolic animals, trees, and numbers, all of which we will explore in this chapter. We will look at other correspondences in later chapters—herbs and essential oils (Chapter 3), crystals (Chapter 4), and lunar phases (Chapter 5).

Next, cleanse and purify your ritual space including your altar and the tools you are using to clear them of any bad energy (see pages 33–36). Think of your ritual tools as energy conductors that absorb and project the energy of the environment and the ritual work you perform. So, keep them clean, clear, and positive. Continue to focus on your intention while you are clearing energy in your space. You must also clear out the clutter in your mind. If you are in a state of inner chaos, the outcome will simply not measure up to your expectations. See pages 37–39 for some suggested practices for centering yourself before you begin your ritual work.

Having finished your preparation, you are now ready to cast a magic circle (see page 41) and start performing spellwork!

setting your intention

Before you craft any spells, it is important to think about what you need. Your reason is your intention, and is the focus of your ritual; holding this in mind will direct your personal energy. I learned the art of intention-setting some years ago and quickly incorporated it into my morning rituals. Upon waking, sometimes even before I open my eyes, I set my intention for the day—it only takes a minute! Your intention can be about anything—work, financial challenges, relationships, health, hopes and dreams.

Rituals may be complex and dramatic, or they may be as simple as floating a single blossom on the surface of a bowl of water. What matters is your intention as you perform your action. Being aware of your magical intentions and the meaning behind your practice brings a deeper significance to your actions. This all leads to greater self-understanding and it is also a way to discover the world around you.

intention-setting tips

- Avoid using words with any negative charge to them, such as "can't," "but," and "won't," and amplify your intention with a statement of gratitude immediately after.
- Always state your intention as if it is happening now and not in the future. Be specific and intend without limit.
- Your intentions do not always have to be personal to you and your loved ones. Intending for the greater good of all contributes to a positive global shift.
- By setting intentions every day, you will soon become a master manifestor. I intend that for you!

clearing energetic clutter

Before you can do any ritual work, you must first clear the energetic clutter that can create blocks. As well as physically clearing the area using your broom (see pages 18–19), there are various other ways to purify a space. We'll explore a few options over the following pages.

One method is to make an energy-clearing lavender-and-mint tea by boiling fresh water and adding 4 sprigs each of fresh lavender and fresh mint. (If you don't have access to the fresh herbs, use 1 teaspoon of each dried herb instead.) Steep for at least 4 minutes, and as long as 10 minutes if there is a lot of energetic clutter. Leave it to cool, then dip your finger in the tea and sprinkle it throughout your home while reciting the following words:

Clean and clear, nothing negative near.

Only healing and helpful energies here.

With harm to none. So mote it be.

Repeat three times, and if you feel the need to clear out any remaining cloud of psychic clutter, add the diluted tea to your cleaner when you wash floors or surfaces. The scent of calm and clarity will lift the spirits of all who enter your space.

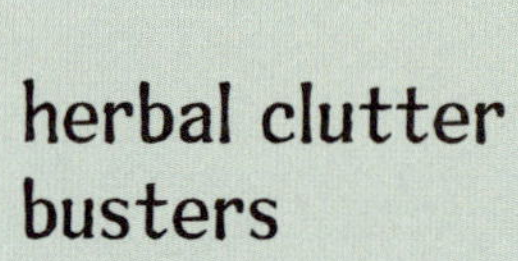

herbal clutter busters

Another way to clear a space of bad energy is with incense. There are lots of different types available. Here are a few ideas but I encourage you to experiment and see what works for you!

sweetgrass

For centuries, many Indigenous communities in North America have burned braided sheaves of sweetgrass, a hardy aromatic herb that grows in the northern hemisphere. It is so beautifully scented that it can also be wafted around unlit as a wand to clear energy. This powerful herb cleanses body, soul, and home, but the highest use is for rituals, when it can be burned to call forth the ancestors and send away anything unwanted.

Sweetgrass can also be brewed into a tea to use as an astringent rinse for body and hair; you can do this by steeping 1 tablespoon of the dried chopped sweetgrass for 5 minutes in a standard teakettle or 4 cups (900 ml) of boiling water. Sweetgrass is also used as an adornment, woven into braids or as a crown.

copal

Mexican and South American healers and modern shamans gather the resin of the copal tree to use as ceremonial incense throughout the year. You will still smell the sweet, pungent smoke of copal in communities that celebrate the Day of the Dead, as it helps us to connect with our ancestors and loved ones who have passed to the other side. Burning copal is part of the ritual, but shamans and healers believe that it also helps to tap and cross over into the spiritual realm. Copal also has the power to bring total relaxation.

palo santo

This dried wood from a tree native to Central and South America plays an important role in South American cultures, where it is burned to clear a space of bad energy. It also activates a higher power in those who use it. Its scent clears out psychic clutter and purifies both you and your environment. It is said that it can literally burn away negative thoughts in your mind—a deeply powerful experience.

smudging

One of the greatest tools for purification is sage, and, while every metaphysical store has it in quantity, I highly recommend gathering or growing it yourself. Aromatic sage dries quickly and can be bound into thick "smudge sticks," which you should keep at the ready in a fireproof clay dish. To make a smudge stick, bind dried sage leaves into bundles with thread wound nine times around and knotted at each loop. Leave room for a handle at the base of the wand, where you wind and knot the threads thrice more. This will honor the Three Fates, who hold the thread of our destiny in their hands: Clotho, who spins the thread of life; Lachesis, who chooses its length and outcome; and Atropos, who cuts the thread.

Use your smudge stick any time purification is in order, especially if you've moved home, started a new job, bought a new car, or purchased any secondhand clothing or furniture. This will help to remove any energy that might be clinging from the previous owner or incumbent. If you have just performed a big decluttering in your home or office, you can further cleanse your personal space by smudging it with sage smoke.

Light your smudge stick and, moving clockwise, circle the area or objects to be purified. Speak these words aloud:

Great Spirit goddess so wise, with this smoke,
Your blessed protection I invoke.
Out with the bad, in with the good.
Harm to none and blessings to all.

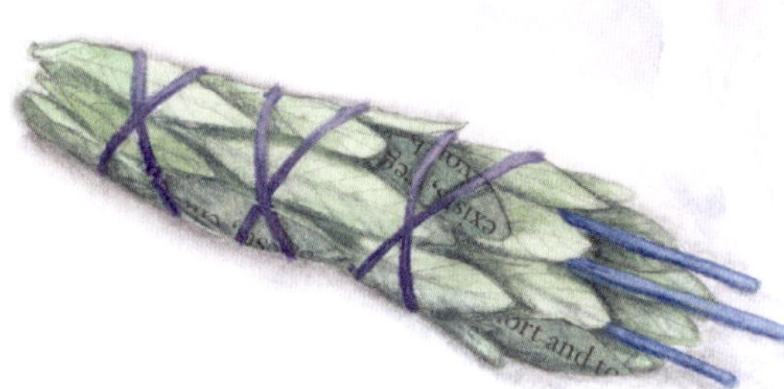

center yourself

To prepare for personal ritual, it is important to center yourself. I call this "doing a readjustment," and I believe this is especially important in our overscheduled and busy world. Doing a readjustment helps pull you back into yourself and gets your priorities on track again. Only when you are truly centered can you do the genuine inner work of self-development that is at the core of ritual. Centering takes many forms. Experiment on your own to find out what works best for you. My priestess pal Kat, for example, does a quick meditation that she calls the "chakra check-in."

the chakra check-in

The chakra system comprises energy points in the astral body—an energetic aura attached to your physical body that is associated with various endocrine glands in the physical

body. See opposite for information about the seven main chakras. By working with your chakras, you can become much more in touch with your body and soul.

To perform this meditation, sit lotus-fashion (with legs crossed, feet on thighs), close your eyes, and visualize the light and color of each of the seven chakras. (If you are on a bus or about to attend a meeting, you can do this exercise just sitting down, feet on the floor.) Bring to mind each chakra and mentally run energy up and down your spine, from bottom to top, pausing at each chakra point. Do this a few times until you feel a soothing calm surrouning you.

I have seen my friend perform her chakra check-in at trade shows and in hotel lobbies, surrounded by the hubbub of many people. She is an ocean of calm at the center of a storm. Prior to performing a spell or magical ritual, try the chakra check-in to calm yourself. Alternatively, perform the centering exercise below.

centering exercise

Take a comfortable sitting position and find your pulse. Keep your fingers on your pulse until you feel the steady rhythm of your own heart. Now begin slowly breathing, in rhythm with your heartbeat. Inhale for four beats, hold for four beats, and then exhale for five beats. Repeat this pattern for six cycles. People have reported that although it seems hard to match up with the heartbeat at first, with a little bit of practice, your breath and heartbeat will synchronize. Your entire body will relax as you are filled with calm.

the seven chakras

- **The crown chakra** at the very top of your head is your connection to the universe, and is violet in color.
- **The third eye chakra** is located in the center of your forehead and is associated with intuition, and the color indigo.
- **The throat chakra** is considered the center of communication, and is blue in color.
- **The heart chakra** in the center of your chest is the emotional center, for all strong feelings from love and happiness to the opposite. It is also associated with spiritual development, the higher self, and the color green.
- **The solar plexus chakra** at the bottom of the breastbone is associated with personal power, and the color yellow.
- **The sacral chakra** is in the abdominal region, just below the navel, and corresponds to such physical urges as hunger and sex, and the color orange.
- **The root chakra** is at the base of your spine and is associated with passion, survival and security, and the color red.

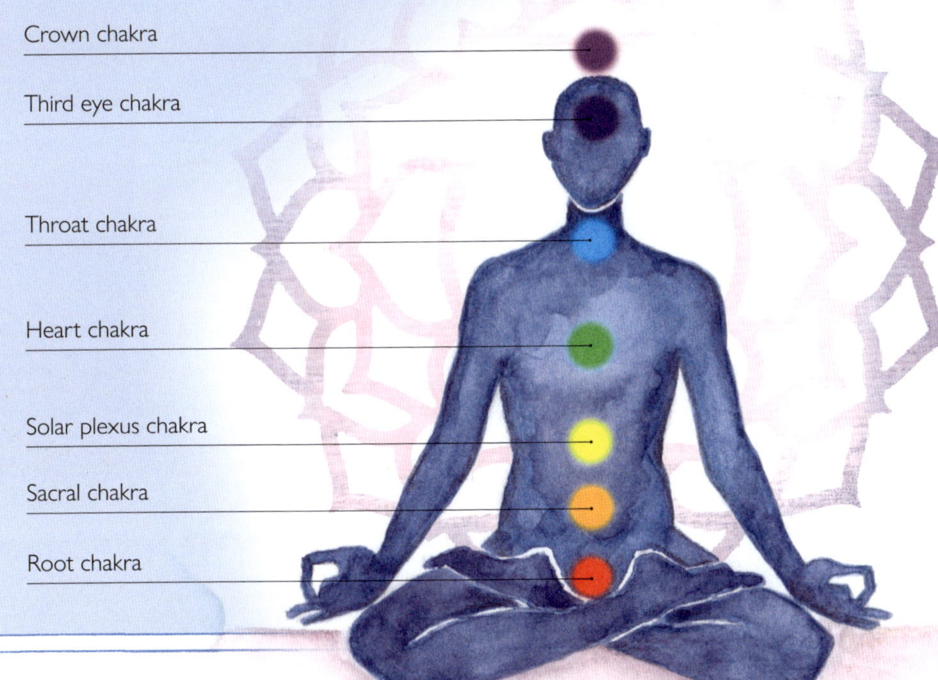

inspired clarity: breath of the gods incense

Burn this mixture of incense on your altar to generate a positive and peaceful atmosphere to set the stage for your ritual. Rose hips and mint are for heart, enthusiasm, and keen thinking. The yellow candle, yellow rose, and the yellow citrine crystal are used to symbolize intelligence and mental clarity.

GATHER TOGETHER

pestle and mortar

1 tablespoon dried rose hips

1 teaspoon fresh or dried mint

piece of charcoal in a fireproof clay or glass dish

yellow candle anointed with neroli essential oil

single yellow rose

vase

1 cup (240 ml) fresh water in a bowl

citrine crystal

Use the pestle and mortar to grind together the rose hips and the mint. Once they are nicely mixed, place the herbs on the piece of charcoal in the fireproof dish. Light the candle and place the yellow rose in the vase to one side of the incense burner. On the other side, place the bowl of water with the citrine crystal in it. Light the incense and breathe in. The word "inspire" comes from the Greek word for "breath of the gods," so allow this divine essence to fill you with grace.

CITRINE

casting a magic circle

A magic circle is created by "casting," or drawing in the air with concentrated energy. You could use your wand or athame to do this. Many a witch casts a circle at the beginning of any spellwork. Inside this circle, energy is raised, rituals are performed, and spells are worked. This consecrated space is also where you call upon the gods and goddesses and become attuned to your own special deities.

With attention and focus, working in the circle can be a wonderfully intense experience. All your senses will come alive. You will feel, see, and hear the energies you invoke. You will have created a tangible sphere of power. When you create a magic circle and use your magical tools in it, you are leaving behind the mundane. Despite the hurly-burly of the daily world, you can touch the sacrosanct.

You can, and doubtlessly will, cast a circle anywhere—out in the forest, on a beach, or in the comfort of your home. Wherever the circle is cast, that space becomes your temple. Wiccan tradition specifies that the circle must have a diameter of 9 feet (2.75 m). We urban pagans might have less space, so you can extend into the closest room. I have had kitchens that more closely resembled large closets, so I would expand into the dining area and living room. The more rooms that are blessed, the better, I say! When you work outdoors with a large group of people, very large group circles are cast.

working with candles

Candles are simple but powerful magical tools, which can be incorporated into all kinds of rituals and spells. They are often chosen for their color correspondences (see pages 44–45)—many of the rituals in this book suggest using specific candle colors.

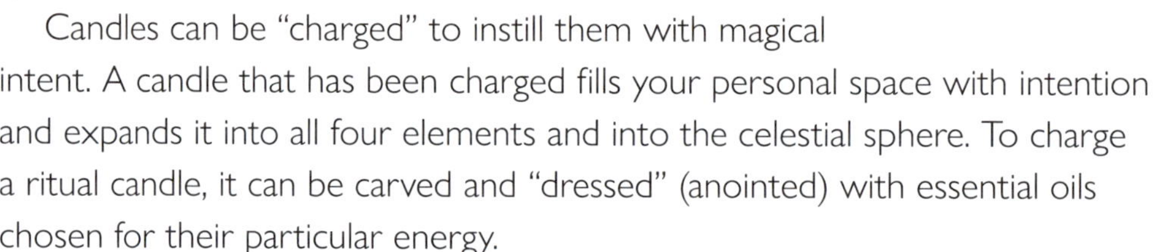

Candles can be "charged" to instill them with magical intent. A candle that has been charged fills your personal space with intention and expands it into all four elements and into the celestial sphere. To charge a ritual candle, it can be carved and "dressed" (anointed) with essential oils chosen for their particular energy.

First, clarify your intention (see page 32) then cleanse your candles by passing them through the purifying smoke of sage or incense (see pages 34–36). Next, warm the tip of your bolline (see page 21) using a lit match and carve your full intention into the candle wax. (Alternatively, you could carve a symbol of your intention or the main words, such as "better health," "more money," or "new love.") As you do so, you are charging it with energy and the hope and purpose of your spell.

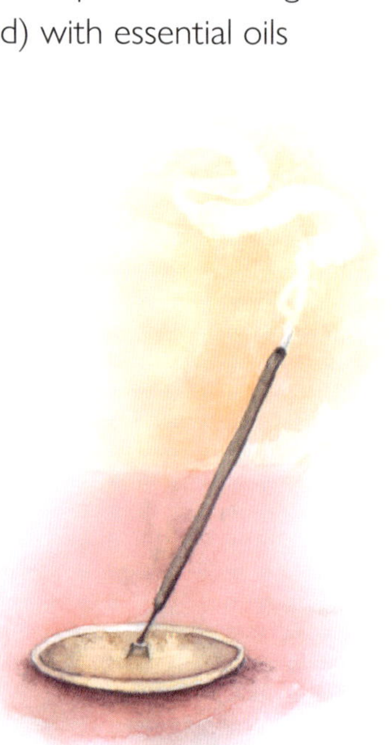

Some highly successful examples that I have used and witnessed are:

- "Healing for my friend who is in the hospital; she will recover with renewed and increased health."
- "I get the raise I am asking for, and more!"
- "New true love enters my life in the coming season, blessed be."

Then, you should "dress" your candle with a couple of drops of essential oil on the side of the candle using a dropper or cotton ball. Every essential oil is imbued with a power that comes from the plants and flowers of which it is made. You can also use oils to anoint yourself at the crown of the head or at the third eye (located between the eyebrows) to increase mental clarity. By using the inherent powers of essential oils and anointing both your tool and yourself, you are increasing the energies of both. See pages 74–79 to find out more about choosing and using essential oils, including safety information.

candle color correspondences

green

Money, prosperity, growth, luck, jobs, gardening, youth, beauty, and fertility.

dark blue

Change, flexibility, the unconscious, psychic powers, and emotional healing.

pink

Love, friendship, kindness, faithfulness, goodness, and affection.

brown

Home, animal wisdom, grounding, and physical healing.

black

Banishes, absorbs, expels the negative, and heals serious illness.

gold

Solar magic, money, attraction, and the astral plane.

orange

The law of attraction, success with legal issues, mutability, stimulation, support, encouragement, and joy.

light blue

Patience, happiness, triumph over depression, calm, deep understanding, and compassion.

red

Strength, protection, sexuality, vitality, passion, courage, heart, intense feelings of love, good health, and power.

white

Purification, peace, protection from negativity, truth, binding, sincerity, serenity, chastity, gladness, and spirit.

purple

Female power, stress relief, ambition, healing past wounds, goddesshood, and business success.

gray

Neutrality, impasses, and cancellation.

yellow

Mental power and vision, intelligence, clear thinking, study, self-assurance, prosperity, divination, psychism, abundance, wisdom, power of persuasion, charisma, and sound sleep.

the power of crystals

Crystals are used regularly in rituals and spellwork and we'll explore this in more detail in Chapter 4. As an introduction to crystal magic, one simple practice is something I like to call "crystal feng shui," which involves leaving crystals in strategic places around your home to help to accelerate the change you desire. Here are a few placements to try, and the specific results they will bring about:

AMETHYST

- **An amethyst** placed on your nightstand will promote healing and release any negative energy that is clinging to your home.
- **Clusters of jade or yellow "lemon quartz"** on your desk or workspace will activate vibrations of abundance and creativity.
- **A big chunk of citrine** placed on the left-hand side of your desk will bring more money into your home or office.
- **An obsidian ball** can absorb negative energy—try putting it in a dark hallway that feels spooky, or any area where the energy seems very static or low.
- **Rose quartz** can be placed anywhere in your bedroom to make it a place of bliss and unconditional love.

ROSE QUARTZ

CITRINE

blessings and strength: hecate invocation

Hecate, above perhaps all others, is the original goddess of witchcraft. She is also the goddess of night, magic, necromancy, the moon, and ghosts. At "the witching hour of midnight," the power of magic is strongest. This is also the optimal time to call down the goddess known as "queen of the witches" for a power boost of blessings and strength. By honoring her and inviting her into your life, you will receive untold gifts of wisdom, joy, and beauty.

GATHER TOGETHER

large crystal, ideally a geode, amethyst, quartz, or rock crystal

3 candles in sturdy glass votives

image of the goddess

rattle or drum

Place the crystal on your altar, along with the candles and the goddess image, then say the following words:

Blessed one, all sky and earth
and ocean is yours.

May we all be blessed by you.

May we all draw strength
from you.

I sing to thee, bright lady.

I dance for thee, queen of all.

In your honor,

Blessed be.

Now, pick up your rattle or drum and shake or beat it while dancing under the midnight sky.

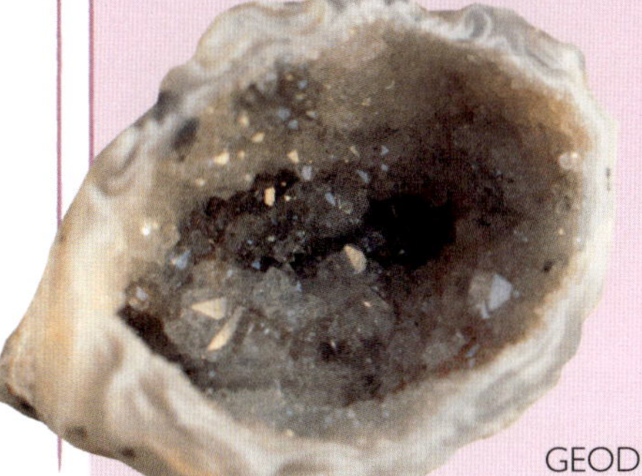

GEODE

elemental magic

Spellwork can allow you to create important changes in your life and to become more connected to the world around you. Wicca is, after all, an earth path, so working in harmony with the elements of which the earth is made is an important step in your personal practice. Earth, air, fire, and water are the four elements of the ancients and were developed during the time of the original pagans. There are very particular powers in the elements you can call on in your ritual work.

earth

Earth is the manifestation of the solid. It is real and tangible matter. The Earth gives us intransigence, constancy, and durability. All beings on this beautiful planet are made of earth, and we are part of a natural, magical system. At the end of our lives, we once again return to the Earth.

Earth is a stable material and element. You should call on the element of earth when you want to become more grounded or to manifest something new and tangible into your life. To embody its presence on your altar, you can grow a flowering plant or place some sand in a shell.

air

Air is the unseen form of matter and is formless, but is ever-changing, possessing mobility and dynamism. The oxygen in the very air we breathe is essential to the continuation of all life on Earth. Wind creates movement and effects change. Rituals invoking the element of air include singing, chanting, and conscious breathing.

fire

Fire is heat and is the most visible form of energy. Fire is a powerful element, as it can transform and change the other elements. If you watch the flicker of your candle flame, the embers of your incense, or the blaze of your fireplace, you will see a constant transmutation of matter. Fire has the ability to both excite and incite us, and fire is necessary to bring about change.

water

Water is the fluid state of matter, the nurturer of all life, and essential for all continued existence. The blood that flows through the veins of animals is mostly water, with trace minerals flowing within it. Water cleanses, nourishes crops, and washes away what no longer serves a purpose.

Water is the opposite of earth in that it flows: it lacks stability. Even ice, water in a stable form, can melt. Water in our rivers, lakes, and oceans is ever-changing. Water is a very important cleansing and blessing element to bring into play in your rituals. A fountain or bowl of water in your home represents the all-important water of life. You can use water for any kind of releasing ritual.

magical intent in your garden

Gardening keeps you grounded with a deep connection to the earth. Your garden—whether it is a balcony full of blooms or a plot out back—can be a sanctuary, a place where your spirit is renewed and restored. Growing herbs to use in remedies and spellcraft is doubly rewarding; with each passing season, you will grow in your wisdom and skill.

Think of all the herbs and plants you love and use often, then begin researching their upkeep and care. Do you use chamomile regularly? Are rosemary, mint, and lavender favorites in your sachets and teas? Do you purify your space with sage? Tending and growing these magical herbs and potent plants is a kind of botanical alchemy; the teas, tinctures, potions, recipes, and flower essences you craft are proof that yours is an enchanted garden. We will explore the magical properties and uses of some specific herbs and plants in detail in Chapter 3.

Make sure to research your planting zone so you get the optimal climate to nurture your plants and herbs. Once you have planned your plantings, infuse your plot with magical intention. Keep careful track of your progress in your Book of Shadows (see page 27). As you grow in experience and expertise, so will the healing power of your plot. Remember to research plants and herbs that can be toxic or poisonous to ensure the safety of children or our canine and feline friends. Many a beloved power flower handed down to us is excellent for magical workings but not at all appropriate for tea or edibles. Make sure children stay far away from wisteria, rhododendron, lily of the valley, narcissus, foxglove, larkspur, hydrangea, and oleander. They are beautiful but deadly, literally.

Every new moon (see page 104) is an opportunity to sow seeds for new beginnings and deepen your magical intent. Your plantings can be a tool you use for a better life, bringing brighter health and greater abundance, as well as mindfulness and serenity. Nature is our greatest teacher and a garden is a gift through which you both give and receive.

rituals for morning and night

With our busy schedules, it can sometimes be hard to find the time for magic. Here are a couple of rituals to try first thing in the morning and last thing at night.

celebration of plenty: morning meditation

True abundance comes from looking at what you have, rather than focusing on what you lack. This spell will begin each day with magic. Upon waking, take time to reflect on the good things in your life. After meditating upon those blessings, say this spell aloud:

Today and every day,
I see the richness of life.
I thank you, Goddess,
For all the gifts and beauty in my world.
Today, I will share my blessings with others and honor you.
I see plenty for all. Blessed be.

awakened breath incantation

Unless you are already a practitioner of magical arts, you may well be casting spells unconsciously that throw obstacles in your path. Negative thoughts can imprint and start to manifest in an unfortunate way.

To clear the way to greater wealth and happiness, go for a walk during the next new moon. Pick up a white stone or white flower and place it on your altar. Light a white candle, and then close your eyes. Empty your mind and breathe deeply. Check to make sure your mind is not wandering; if any negative thoughts are lingering, send them out of your mind permanently.

After ten deep inhales and exhales, you should begin to feel a buzzing at the crown of your head. Now, open your eyes, stare into the flame of the candle, and repeat seven times:

I am alive.

I have power.

It is real.

And so it is.

Any time you find yourself engaged in negative self-talk or thinking, repeat this spell.

every day is sacred

Magic can be performed any time, but each day of the week has certain magical associations. Knowing these is extremely useful for planning the timings of your spellwork for maximum success.

mondays are made for magic

Monday comes from "moon day" and is ruled by the moon goddess known variously as Diana, Cybele, Artemis, and Selene. This first day of the work week is associated with all the hues of blue, from sapphire to pearly iridescent. This is the day for intuition, deep reflection, and love, especially loving your own true nature.

tuesdays are for magical plans

Named after the Norse god, Tiw, Tuesday is ruled by Mars, the god of war and action. This day wears the colors red and pink. Like the old saying, "Tuesday is good news day," this day is auspicious for matters regarding prosperity, truth, new beginnings, and high energy with focus.

wednesday is "we" day

The very word "Wednesday" comes from the old German name for the supreme god, Woden. Woden's day is associated with the winged god of communication, Mercury, whose colors are yellow and green. This is an optimal time for getting together with like-minded folks or making a new contact. Wednesday stands for strength, joy, theatrics, extravagance, and great staying power.

thursdays will bring you good fortune

Named after the Norse god, Thor, Thursday is an excellent day for manifesting. Turn to Thor when you need to use spirituality as an approach to solve a legal matter. He is also a powerful protection deity to invoke in ritual. You can and should do prosperity rituals

every Thursday through prayer and offerings to this ancient god of abundance. Thor is the equivalent of the Greco-Roman god Jupiter, or Jove. These generous deities can always be counted on to deliver. The color of this day is blue.

fridays are festivals

Friday is associated with Venus, the Roman goddess of love, and Freya, the powerful goddess also associated with love in the Norse pantheon. As such, Fridays are the time to get out and be social, whether it be date night, girls' night out, or a lovely dinner with family and friends. Be with people, express yourself, laugh, and be merry.

saturdays are for me-time

Associated with black, white, and gray, Saturday is the day of the ruling judge Saturn. This is when we must take stock of the week, get errands and personal business done, practice self-care, and finish the day off with a decorous meal with loved ones.

sundays are for basking in the warmth

Sunday is the day of our greatest star, Sol, otherwise known as the sun, with colors of gold, orange, and radiant white. This is the time to rest and renew, indulge in creativity, and enjoy the fruits of this life. Sunday is also the time to boost your confidence and to make spells for fame and fortune.

magical correspondences

You can enhance your enchantments with magical correspondences. Trees, animals, and numbers all have different significance and purposes, which we'll explore in this section. Other correspondences (for herbs, essential oils, crystals, and lunar phases) can be found in later chapters.

trees

- **Acacia:** Clairvoyance, divination, visions, wealth, and protection.
- **Alder:** Banishing, transformation, truth, and intuition.
- **Apple:** Dreams, fertility, love, luck, and harmony.
- **Birch:** Protection (especially defensive magic), concentration, and creativity. Alleviates anxiety.
- **Cedar:** Clairvoyance (especially the afterlife) and psychic ability. Alleviates hexes.
- **Cypress:** Protection (especially binding and defensive magic), comfort, mental ability, and wisdom.
- **Elder:** Grounding, healing, love, and success.
- **Elm:** Intuition, love, pregnancy and childbirth, and stability.
- **Juniper:** Fertility, happiness, protection, optimism, and strength.
- **Oak:** Confidence, justice, luck, money, success, independence, and wealth.
- **Pine:** Beginnings, hope, prosperity, and freedom.
- **Rowan:** Devotion, guidance, and psychic ability (especially visions).
- **Willow:** Protection, knowledge, and fertility.
- **Witch hazel:** Healing, inspiration, willpower, fidelity, and wisdom.

animals

- **Bird:** Travel, mental ability (especially memory), and divination.
- **Canary:** Harmony, joy, love, and luck.
- **Cat:** Independence, protection, uncovering secrets, and communication with spirits.
- **Chameleon:** Mutability, invisibility, protection, and power over the weather.
- **Dog:** Loyalty, sustained effort, hearing, friendship, and protection.
- **Fish:** Wealth, family, children, divination, and attraction (especially love).
- **Frog:** Initiation, transformation, and regeneration. Alleviates negative energy and psychic blocks.
- **Lizard:** Dreams (divination) and imagination.
- **Lovebird:** Love (especially marriage, partnership, and companionship).
- **Parrot:** Impersonation and repetition.
- **Snake:** Creativity, wisdom, psychic ability, rebirth and regeneration, and communication with spirits.
- **Spider:** Insight, originality, and new beginnings.
- **Turtle:** Patience, perspicacity, and longevity.

numbers

Numerology is a magical discipline devised millennia ago. The earliest known system was developed by Pythagoras, a Greek philosopher from the sixth century BCE. The Pythagoreans, who were followers of Pythagoras, invested specific numbers with mystical properties. The correspondences listed opposite are based on the ancient Pythagorean system on which modern-day numerology is founded.

The number three is of special significance to Wiccans, because of the three-by-three law (whatever you send out will be returned to you threefold). In numerology, this number is also linked to the threefold nature of divinity, or the Trinity, and to the connection between mind, body, and spirit. The number four invokes the four elements of earth, air, fire, and water and the four directions of north, east, south, and west. The number seven is significant due to the seven chakras of the body (see page 39) and seven heavens, while the number eight signifies infinity.

master numbers

In the Pythagorean tradition, the three master numbers (11, 22, and 33) were thought to have a special power and significance of their own. Eleven is linked to intuition, clairvoyance, and spiritual healing. Twenty-two is connected to the unlimited potential of mastery in any area (spiritual, physical, emotional, and mental). Thirty-three indicates that all things are possible.

numerical correspondences

- **One:** Independence, individuality, new beginnings, self-development, progress, and creativity.
- **Two:** Balance (especially of yin and yang energies), selflessness and dedication (especially to others), attraction (especially between two people), and compromise.
- **Three:** Expansion, expression, communication, fun, self-expression, giving outwardly, openness, and optimism.
- **Four:** Security, foundations, self-discipline (especially of work and service), productivity, organization, and wholeness.
- **Five:** Freedom, action and energy (especially physical), transformation, adventure, resourcefulness, travel, curiosity, impulsiveness, and excitement.
- **Six:** Self-harmony, compassion, love, service (especially to the community), social responsibility, beauty, the arts, generosity, concern, caring, children, and balance.
- **Seven:** Inner life and inner wisdom, birth and rebirth, strength (especially religious), commitment, solitude, analysis, and contemplation.
- **Eight:** Prosperity, power, abundance, cosmic consciousness, reward, authority, and leadership.
- **Nine:** Humanitarianism, selflessness and dedication (especially to others), completion, endings, compassion, tolerance, and wisdom.

1 2 3 4 5 6 7 8 9

CHAPTER THREE

magical ingredients: teas, herbs, and essential oils

Learning about and utilizing the magical properties of natural ingredients, such as plants, herbs, and spices, will greatly enhance your spellwork. Every tea you brew, each seed you plant, and the essential oils you work with will all offer numerous curative powers.

conjuring by the cup

Teas and herbal infusions are not only delectable drinks, but also of equal importance are the great healing powers contained in each cup. Growing and drying herbs for your own brews is truly one of life's simple pleasures. These brews conjure a very powerful alchemy because, when you drink them, you take the magic inside of you.

For an ambrosial brew with the power to calm any storm, add a sliver of ginger root and a teaspoon each of chamomile and peppermint to two cups of boiling water. Let steep and, as the mixture brews and cools, pray using the words below.

This day I pray for strength and health,
And the wisdom to see the beauty in each waking moment.
Blessings abound; good health is true wealth.

blessings on a budget

Instead of composting all the herbs, twigs, and stems from your brews, you can store them in a burlap or muslin sack and allow them to dry. Keep stuffing in twigs of mint, lavender, rosemary, and all the leftover plant material until you have a big bag. Then, on a special evening, burn it in your fireplace or an outdoor bonfire and it will be like a gigantic incense burner with lovely scents wafting from the flames. And the best part? It's one hundred percent free!

healthy herbal teas

Herbal teas nourish the soul, heal the body, and calm the mind. Try any of the following:

- **Blackberry leaf** reduces mood swings and evens glucose levels, thus aiding weight management. This miraculous herbal even helps circulation and aids such issues as inflammation and varicose veins.
- **Cardamom** is a favorite of expectant mothers everywhere as it calms nausea and morning sickness; this fragrant is excellent for digestion and clears and cleans your mouth and throat. Anyone who likes cinnamon will love cardamom.
- **Catnip** is one of the witchiest of teas and is not only grown as fun for your feline familiar. At the first inkling of a sore throat or impending cold, drink a warm cup of catnip tea and head off to bed. You will awaken feeling much better. Catnip soothes the nervous system and is a gentle but potent sleep-inducer.
- **Dandelion root** grounds and centers, providing many minerals and nutrients. This wonderful weed is also a cleanser and a wholly natural detoxifier. It can also be used to call upon spirits—see page 65.
- **Echinacea** lends an increased and consistent sense of well-being and prevents colds and flu. It is a very powerful immune booster and makes the body strong.
- **Fennel** is excellent for awakening and uplifting and is great for digestion and cleansing. It is also a natural breath freshener.
- **Ginger root** calms and cheers while aiding digestion and nausea and can also fend off coughs and sore throats.
- **Nettle** raises your energy levels, boosts the immune system, and is packed with iron and vitamins. It is also good for lung function and hex breaking.

jasmine tea joy ritual

A delightful concoction, jasmine tea can create an aura of bliss and conviviality. It is available at any grocer or purveyor of organic goods, but homegrown is even better. Jasmine is a vine and represents the intertwining of people. You will be more bonded to anyone with whom you share this sweet ritual. This is also a tonic that you can indulge in when alone.

I recommend brewing up a batch every Monday, or "Moon Day," to ensure that each week is filled with joyfulness. As the tea steeps, say the words below. Let the tea cool then add two parts lemonade to one part jasmine tea and drink the mixture with a good friend.

On this Moon Day in this new week,
I call upon the spirits to guide joy to my door.
By this moon on this day, I call upon Selene, goddess fair,
To show me the best way to live.
For this, I am grateful.
Blessed be the brew; blessed be me.

dandelion root telepathy tea

The humble dandelion, abhorred by lawn keepers everywhere, hides its might very well. Dandelion root tea can call upon the spirit of anyone whose advice you might need. Simply place a freshly brewed simple using this herbal root on your bedroom altar or nightstand. Before you sleep, say the name of your helper aloud seven times. In a dream or vision, the spirit will visit you and answer all your questions. During medieval times, this spell was used to find hidden treasure, and English poet Geoffrey Chaucer, who was well-versed in astrology and other metaphysics, advised this tried-and-true tea.

herbal infusions

Many enthusiasts enjoy several cups a day of their favorite herbal infusion, which is a large portion of herb brewed for at least four hours and as long as ten. I recommend one cup of the dried herb placed in a 1-quart (1-liter) canning jar and filled with freshly boiled water. After the steeping, strain using a nonmetallic method, such as cheesecloth or bamboo.

Herbal infusions can be made with the leaves and fruits that provide the magical and healing aspects of this comforting concoction. Many of the favorite kitchen witch herbs contain minerals, antioxidants, and phytochemicals. Roots, leaves, flowers, needles, and seeds can all be used—depending on which fruit or herb is chosen to be the base. There are some cases when all parts of the plant can be used in some manner, and for others only one or two parts are safe—it is important, when creating a blend from scratch, to research the ingredients to understand what parts can be used.

What do you need to attend to in your life right now? Opposite, I've listed some of the most popular herbs and fruits—and their associations—that are used to create infusions, which you can try in addition to the herbal teas listed on page 63. One of the smartest ways to create an infusion is to brew right before bedtime and you will awaken to a freshly infused herb.

herbs for infusion and their associations

- **Anise seeds and leaves** soothe cramps and aches.
- **Caraway seeds** aid in romantic issues.
- **Chamomile flowers** help with sleep and are good for abundance.
- **Dandelion leaves** make wishes come true.
- **Ginseng root** increases men's vigor.
- **Peppermint leaves** rid tummy discomfort and are cleansing.
- **Pine needles** increase skin health as well as financial health.
- **Rose hip fruit** is packed with vitamin C and can halt colds and flu.
- **Sage leaves** purify energy and are a natural antibiotic.
- **Skullcap leaves** can cure insomnia, headaches, anxiety, and nervous tension.
- **St. John's wort leaves** act as an antidepressant and provide protection.
- **Thyme leaves** are antiseptic and a protectant.
- **Yarrow flowers** reduce fever and bring courage and good luck.

easy plant magic

I am lucky indeed to have had my Aunt Edith, who was a gardener and herbalist. She had the greenest of thumbs and taught me everything I know about gardening. She was very patient and kindly taught me which wild plants were safe to eat and which sign of the moon was best for certain plants, as well as when to use this esoteric, albeit irresistible and fascinating, knowledge in magical workings. With her encouragement, I developed my knowledge of how to make the most of the herbs, nuts, and flowers in the garden and the kitchen cupboard. Here are just a few quick fixes for instant results.

Alfalfa: Put a stalk in a small jar in the cupboard or pantry to ward off poverty.

Allspice: Burn ground allspice to attract luck and fortune, or use in herbal baths for healing.

Almond: Make offerings of almonds to the deities when you or loved ones need a speedy recovery.

Aloe: Grow aloe in or around your home to prevent accidents or illness.

Bay leaf: Write a healing wish on a bay leaf and place it on your altar overnight.

Bayberry: Burn a white candle sprinkled with bayberry oil for good fortune and money.

Black cohosh: Use a cup of cool black cohosh tea as a hair rinse to restore your focus.

Carnation: Add 12 carnation flowers to your bathwater for blooming health.

Chamomile: Tuck a chamomile teabag into your pillowcase for deep, sweet sleep.

Cumin: Add cumin to a goblet of wine for a spicy love spell.

Dandelion: Carry this herb in your pocket to bring luck in love and money.

Echinacea: Wash your hands in cool echinacea tea for greater physical strength.

Fennel: Both as a food ingredient and garden herb, fennel brings longevity.

Gardenia: In potpourri and as an essential oil, gardenia promotes peace of mind.

Ginseng: Carve a wish into a ginseng root and throw it into water to make the wish come true.

Hawthorn: Wash floors with an infusion of hawthorn to remove negative energies.

Honeysuckle: Crush the flowers and rub them into your forehead to enhance psychic powers.

Ivy: Encircle a yellow candle with ivy at the base and burn it for a day to repair a relationship.

Jasmine: Wear a crown of jasmine vine for prophetic visions and new ideas.

Lavender: Dried lavender flowers in a pouch under your pillow will help heal depression.

Marjoram: Use an infusion in the bath for seven days to aid in resolving sadness or grief.

Mint: Stuff a green doll figure with dried mint leaves to heal yourself or a loved one.

Mullein: Burn mullein to banish bad vibrations and bring a quick halt to bad habits.

Parsley: Use parsley in spells to increase strength and vitality after surgery or illness.

Poppy: Place dried poppy seeds into a pouch under your pillow to cure insomnia.

Rose: Rose petals in a bath help bruises and sprains heal much more quickly.

Rosemary: Wash your hands with an infusion of rosemary before any healing rituals for purification.

Sage: Burning sage is essential for self-purification and very helpful for recovering from grief and loss because it shifts energy in a positive way.

Spearmint: A ritual bath made with a cup of crushed spearmint leaves helps the lungs.

Violet: This flower of peace can be used in serenity spells.

herbs for your altar

You can create a scented sachet of herbs aligned with your desire and place it on your altar. Here are some ideas:

- **Cinnamon** refreshes and directs spirituality. A protection herb, it is also handy for healing, money, love, sensuality, personal power, and success with work and creativity.
- **Clove** is good for bringing money and for helping evade and block negative energies.
- **Lavender** is a potent healer that calms and aids deep rest and dreams.
- **Myrrh** has been considered to be very sacred since ancient times and will intensify your spirituality. It also wards off bad spirits.
- **Nutmeg** is a lucky herb that promotes good health and abundance. It also encourages loyalty and marital fidelity.
- **Peppermint** is a herb of purification and increases psychic powers. Mint brings relaxation and can help you sleep, reducing anxiety.
- **Rosemary** purifies and increases memory and intelligence. This savory plant heightens sensuality and bonds of love. It will also keep you youthful!
- **Sage** brings wisdom, health, and a long life. It is very useful for dispelling negative vibrations and encouraging cleansing.
- **Star anise** aids divination and psychic abilities.
- **Tonka bean** will give you courage and draws love and money.
- **Vanilla** is a herb of love and expands and enriches your mental capacity.

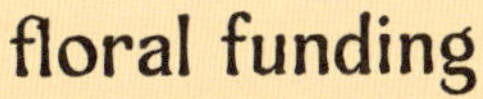

floral funding

The following list of plants can be used in any ritual work whose intention is prosperity. Try these alone or in mixtures, tinctures, or grind into your incenses. You can also plant a prosperity garden and refresh your abundance altar with herbs and flowers grown by your own hand.

- Allspice
- Almond
- Basil
- Bergamot
- Cedar leaves
- Cinnamon
- Cinquefoil
- Clover
- Dill
- Ginger
- Heliotrope
- Honeysuckle
- Hyssop

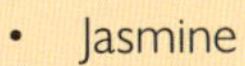

- Jasmine
- Mint
- Myrtle
- Nutmeg
- Oakmoss
- Sassafras
- Vervain
- Woodruff

power potpourri

Whenever you feel the need to infuse your space with protection or want an energetic turnaround from negative to positive, simmer this mixture in a pot of water on your stove. A bad day at work, family squabble, an unfortunate incident in your neighborhood—instead of just muddling along, you can do something about it, and your creation of the positive will help you and your loved ones as well as your neighbors. This power potpourri will also safeguard you from outside influences that can be disruptive. Set your intention before gathering the herbs from your stores.

GATHER TOGETHER

¼ cup (15 g) dried rosemary

⅛ cup (5 g) dried sage

4 dried bay laurel leaves

1 teaspoon dried juniper berries

mixing bowl

pot or pan of simmering water

Mix the herbs together by hand. While you are sifting them through your fingers, close your eyes and visualize your home protected by a boundary of glowing white light. Imagine the light running through you to the herbs in your hand and charging them with the energy of safety, sanctity, and protection. Add the herbs to the pot of slowly simmering water and breathe in the newly charged air.

handmade herbal amulets

Growing your own herbs can be a source of great enjoyment. One way of sharing that pleasure with those you love is by creating and gifting herbal amulets. Amulets are intended to be kept on your person at all times, whether in a pocket, purse, or book bag, or on a string around your neck.

I keep a stock of small muslin drawstring bags for creating amulets. If you are crafty, you can make the bags, sewing them by hand, and stuff the dried herbs inside. The list below offers some suggested herbs and intentions for your amulets.

- **An acorn** for youthful looks.
- **Comfrey** for safe travels.
- **Cyclamen or mistletoe** for fertility.
- **Ivy, broomstraw, or maidenhair fern** for fellow witches.
- **Mugwort** for strength.
- **Mullein or borage** for courage and heart.
- **Nettle or yarrow** for good cheer.
- **Rue** for good health.
- **Snapdragon** for protection from deceit.
- **Woodruff** for success.

essential oils

The global embrace of essential oils, and their healing and calming properties, is endlessly pleasing to me. Essential oils are highly concentrated extracts of flowers, herbs, roots, or resins. One of the biggest trends the world over, people simply love essential oils for the uplifting scent and serenity they bring. These plant-powered essences are immensely useful in so many ways—see the at-a-glance guide opposite. Try to ensure you are using natural oils instead of manufactured, chemical-filled perfume oil; the synthetics lack any real energy.

safety first

Approach oils with caution and don't get them in your eyes. Wearing clean cotton gloves is a good idea and you can avoid any mess by using oil droppers. Do not use essential oils in the first trimester of pregnancy and consult a health professional if using in the later stages. Essential oils should never be applied directly to the skin—they must first be blended with a carrier, or base, oil (see pages 76–77) to dilute the essential oil and make it safe to apply to the skin. Always test a blend on a small area of the skin first and leave for 24 hours to check you don't have any reaction to it. Find a trusted herbalist or the wise sage at your local metaphysical shop for further advice; usually they can offer much in the way of helpful knowledge.

quick and easy aromatherapy

Essential oils have aromatic molecules that pass through the blood–brain barrier. This has a direct effect on the parts of our brain that control our state of anxiety, stress, and sadness. Application of these helpful essential oils to alleviate most negative emotions and moods can be quick and simple.

- Breathing in relief: Drop one or two drops of blended oil into the palm of your hand and slowly breath in the scent.
- Pulse points: Put two drops of blended oil onto a cotton ball and gently touch it to your temples and wrists to unwind.
- Diffuse tension: Diffusers are popular in homes and offices as they simply emanate serenity. For tranquility when you're on the move, a couple of drops of blended oil on a scarf around your neck will ease your way.
- Medicinal mist: Plug the drain in your shower and turn on the hot water, then add five drops of blended oil. Let it run for a few minutes, then hop in and breathe in deeply.

The following classic oils are excellent choices:

- Bergamot
- Eucalyptus
- Geranium
- Peppermint
- Rosemary
- Tea tree
- Thyme

carrier oils

A carrier oil, also known as a base oil, is a vegetable- or plant-based oil that is used to dilute essential oils without diminishing the effect of the essence. This is to ensure essential oils used topically are safe to apply to the skin. Carrier oils support the curative power of essential oils and can also be a vessel for healing in themselves. The box opposite lists some different carrier oils and their properties.

For a simple relaxation massage oil blend, add up to 18 drops of essential oil(s) to ½ cup (120 ml) of carrier oil in a dark-colored, sealable bottle. (Try an equal mix of sandalwood, lavender, and clary sage oils with jojoba or almond oil.) Carefully cap the bottle and gently shake until the oils have blended together. Store the bottle in a dark cupboard. Before using it on yourself or a loved one, shake well. You can warm it by putting the sealed bottle in a cup of warm water and let it sit there for 4 minutes. Many masseuses pour the oil into their palm and let their own body heat warm it.

almond oil

This comes from the almond tree and is one of the carrier oils that can blend seamlessly with any other oil. It corresponds with Mercury, brightens the mind and mood, and is wonderful as a topical healer.

apricot kernel oil

Imbued with sweetness and a warm energy, this strength-giving essence is especially good for women, nurturing them at every age and stage of life. Apricot kernel oil also protects love.

coconut oil

This oil is very thick and emanates a splendid fragrance that is immediately heartening. It is an emollient that not only soothes and heals skin and minor abrasions, but also has the magical properties of cleansing and purifying. It is associated with the element of water.

evening primrose oil

This oil speeds the healing of bruises and wounds, and is extremely good for women, including helping with labor and easing pregnancy discomforts. Evening primrose abets clairvoyance and paranormal gifts. It will help you to see clearly.

grape-seed oil

Packed with vitamin E, this is fantastic for applying oils to your skin. It also augments spiritual growth. This should be one of the oils that you turn to for anointing yourself or any statues of gods and goddesses before rituals.

jojoba oil

This oil absorbs extremely well into the skin, supporting and blending with anything it is mixed with. It is also a remarkable anointing oil. Jojoba should be used in recipes and rituals that help to deal with depression and support perseverance in hardship.

olive oil

Connected to the element of fire, this oil is imbued with warmth and comfort. It was named "liquid gold" by the ancient Greek poet Homer, and rightly so—the healing properties have been greatly valued for millennia, as have the benefits to women, even increasing fertility. It is associated with vitality, money, success, and joyfulness.

sesame oil

A simply marvelous oil for your skin, sesame oil is absorbed lightly and easily. It is very rich in vitamins E and B, and in minerals which include calcium, magnesium, and phosphorus. It is an excellent emollient, and makes for a very pleasing massage oil.

sunflower oil

Permeated with the energy of our sun, this oil is powerful and life-giving. Use it when you desire rapid growth and amplification of positive energy. Sunflower oil brings wisdom and is a protector.

magical meanings of essential oils

Knowing which essential oils to use in your spells is vital to your craft. This list matches the intention of your spell to various essences, but you can also match the essence to qualities you want to bring to your personal space.

- **Astral projection:** Benzoin, cinnamon, jasmine, sandalwood.
- **Courage:** Black pepper, frankincense, geranium.
- **Dispelling negative energy and spirits:** Basil, clove, copal, frankincense, juniper, myrrh, peppermint, pine, rosemary, Solomon's seal, vervain, yarrow.
- **Divination:** Camphor, clove, orange.
- **Enchantment:** Amber, apple, ginger, tangerine.
- **Healing:** Bay, cedarwood, cilantro (coriander), cinnamon, eucalyptus, juniper, lime, rose, sandalwood, spearmint.
- **Joy:** Bergamot, lavender, neroli, vanilla.
- **Love:** Basil, chamomile, cilantro (coriander), clove, copal, geranium, jasmine, lemon, lime, neroli, rose, rosemary, ylang-ylang.
- **Luck:** Nutmeg, orange, rose, vervain.
- **Peace:** Chamomile, lavender.
- **Prosperity:** Aloe, basil, cinnamon, clove, ginger, nutmeg, oakmoss, orange, patchouli, peppermint, pine.
- **Protection:** Anise, bay, black pepper, cedarwood, clove, copal, cypress, eucalyptus, frankincense, juniper, lavender, lime, myrrh, rose geranium, sandalwood, vetiver.
- **Sexuality:** Amber, cardamom, clove, lemongrass, olive, patchouli, rose.

find your celestial essence

Every plant corresponds with certain planetary energies. Synergize with your astrological chart by trying the essential oils that match your sun sign and your moon sign, perhaps even in combination, in your magical and healing workings.

- Aries, ruled by Mars: Carnation, cedar, clove, juniper, peppermint, pine.
- Taurus, ruled by Venus: Apple, lilac, oakmoss, orchid, plumeria, rose, vanilla, violet.
- Gemini, ruled by Mercury: Bergamot, lavender, lemongrass, lily, peppermint.
- Cancer, ruled by the Moon: Eucalyptus, gardenia, jasmine, lemon, myrrh, sandalwood.
- Leo, ruled by the Sun: Acacia, cinnamon, orange, rosemary.
- Virgo, ruled by Mercury: Bergamot, cypress, patchouli, spearmint.
- Libra, ruled by Venus: Catnip, marjoram, mugwort, spearmint, sweet pea, vanilla.
- Scorpio, ruled by Pluto: Allspice, basil, galangal, ginger.
- Sagittarius, ruled by Jupiter: Anise, cedarwood, honeysuckle.
- Capricorn, ruled by Saturn: Lemon thyme, mimosa, vervain, vetiver.
- Aquarius, ruled by Uranus: Citron, cypress, lavender, pine, spearmint.
- Pisces, ruled by Neptune: Neroli, orris, sweet pea.

CHAPTER FOUR

crystal power: sacred stones and gems

Using gems and crystals in rituals, spells, and affirmations has been part of the human experience for millennia. With crystal magic, you will learn to improve your life in ways large and small.

an introduction to crystals

Every crystal and gemstone has many correspondences and enhancing abilities. While one may offer protection and healing (useful against illness), another may offer protection and courage (ideal for facing your fears), so choose your stone wisely and ensure it is a good fit for the intentions of your spell. Make a note of which correspondences work best for you so you can keep track of your results and learn as you go.

AGATE

Agate: Courage, strength, love, and protection.

Alexandrite: Luck, love, spiritual transformation, and joy.

Amazonite: Success, joy, and self-expression.

Amber: Transformation (especially negative energy into positive energy) and protection.

APACHE TEAR

Amethyst: Courage, psychic energy, dream control and recall, addiction (healing), intuition, peace, happiness, and love.

Apache tear: Protection and luck.

Aquamarine: Courage, purification, peace, psychic energy, and self-expression.

AZURITE

Azurite: Psychic energy, divination, healing, concentration, and transformation.

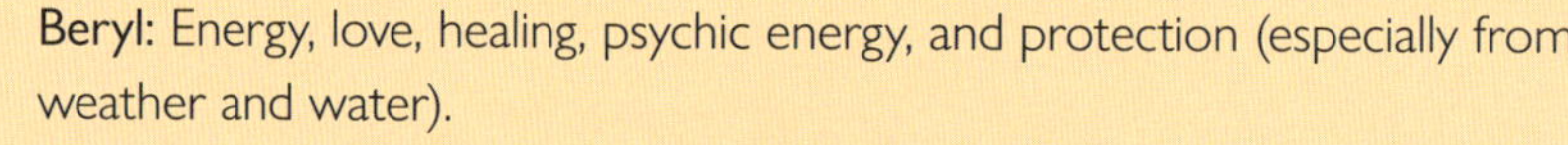

Beryl: Energy, love, healing, psychic energy, and protection (especially from weather and water).

CALCITE

Bloodstone: Courage, strength, victory, wealth, self-confidence, and success (especially in business and legal affairs).

Calcite: Centering, grounding, purification, money, and peace. Alleviates fear.

Carnelian: Courage, sexual energy, communication (especially verbal), and peace. Alleviates jealousy, apathy, fear, and rage.

CARNELIAN

Celestite: Communication (especially verbal), healing, compassion, and growth. Alleviates stress.

Chrysocolla: Wisdom, peace, love, communication, and vitality.

CHRYSOPRASE

Chrysoprase: Prosperity, luck, happiness, friendship, protection, and healing.

Citrine: Balance, psychic energy, protection, creativity, and sexual energy. Alleviates nightmares.

Clear quartz: Energy and protection.

Coral: Protection (especially from conflict).

DIAMOND

Diamond: Courage, strength, healing, and protection.

Emerald: Prosperity, dream control and recall, meditation, love, peace, and balance.

Fluorite: Balance and stability (especially in relationships).

GARNET

Garnet: Strength, healing, protection, purification, and compassion.

Geode: Fertility, childbirth, meditation, dream control and recall, and astral travel.

Hematite: Grounding, calming, healing, divination, intuition, and relaxation (especially sleep).

HEMATITE

Herkimer diamond: Psychic ability and clairvoyance.

Infinite: Communication (especially with angels).

Iolite: Accuracy and psychic ability (especially visions).

Jade: Healing, protection, wisdom, prosperity, love, longevity, fertility, and peace.

IOLITE

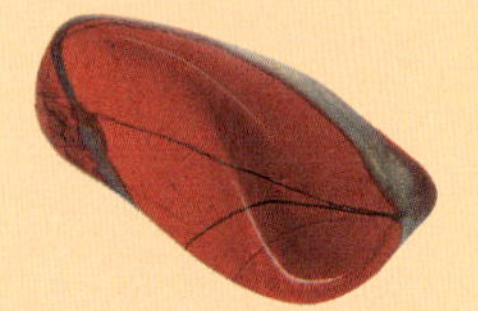

JASPER

LEPIDOLITE

MOONSTONE

OPAL

PERIDOT

ROSE QUARTZ

Jasper: Healing, protection, health, beauty, and energy.

Jet: Protection (especially from hexes). Alleviates fear.

Kunzite: Creativity, balance, communication, grounding, and relaxation.

Kyanite: Emotional balance.

Lapiz lazuli: Courage, creativity, joy, love, fidelity, protection, healing, beauty, and prosperity.

Lepidolite: Peace, spirituality, luck, protection, psychic ability, and emotional balance. Alleviates nightmares.

Lodestone: Cleansing.

Malachite: Power, energy, protection, love, peace, and success (especially in business and gardening).

Marble: Protection, dream recall, and meditation.

Moldavite: Psychic ability and emotional balance.

Moonstone: Grounding, love, divination, relaxation (especially sleep), protection, harmony, peace, youthfulness, and fortune (especially in gardening and travel).

Obsidian: Grounding, divination, and protection. Alleviates negativity.

Onyx: Emotional balance, self-control, binding, protection, and strength.

Opal: Beauty, prosperity, luck, power, psychic abilities, and emotional balance.

Pearl: Peace, serenity, and truthfulness.

Peridot: Protection, prosperity, relaxation (especially sleep), health, emotional balance, and intuition.

Rhodochrosite: Energy, peace, calm, love, and emotional balance.

Rose quartz: Love, peace, happiness, and healing.

Ruby: Prosperity, power, courage, integrity, and joy. Alleviates nightmares.

RUBY

Rutilated quartz: Communication.

Sapphire: Psychic abilities, inspiration, love, meditation, peace, healing, power, prosperity, and protection.

Smoky quartz: Healing and transformation. Alleviates negative energy.

SMOKY QUARTZ

Sodalite: Healing, meditation, wisdom, calm, and grounding. Alleviates stress.

Sugilite: Love and harmony. Alleviates negative energy.

Sunstone: Protection, energy, health, passion, and sexuality.

SUNSTONE

Tektite: Enhancement (especially of energy) and enlightenment.

Tiger's eye: Courage, prosperity, protection, energy, luck, judgment and common sense, honesty, and divination. Alleviates depression.

Topaz: Protection, healing, prosperity, love, emotional balance, tranquility, and creativity.

TOPAZ

Tourmaline: Love, friendship, prosperity, business, peace, relaxation (especially sleep), energy, courage, protection, and inspiration.

Turquoise: Courage, protection, prosperity, luck, friendship, healing, communication, happiness, emotional balance, and astral travel.

TURQUOISE

Unakite: Power and transformation (especially negative energy into positive energy).

Zircon: Protection, beauty, love, peace, sexual energy, healing, alertness, and emotional balance.

ZIRCON

crystal cleansing salt spell

The first thing you need to do when you get a new crystal is to cleanse it so it does not shed any potentially negative vibrations from others. This can be done with a simple salt ritual.

GATHER TOGETHER

1 cup (200 g) sea salt

glass bowl

crystal to be cleansed

black candle

matches

sage bundle (see page 36)

fireproof dish

Add the salt to the glass bowl and put your crystal on top of the salt. Light the black candle, then light the sage from the candle flame and put it in the fireproof dish. Speak this spell:

Bone of the earth, filled with
ancient power,

Filled with grounding,
filled with healing.

Let go of all that came before.

You are now here.

You are welcome here.

With harm to none, and blessings to all.

Roll the crystal so every side touches the salt and then repeat the spell. Snuff both the sage and the candle and let the stone rest in the salt overnight. In the morning, remove the crystal and let it power up on your altar to become imbued with your energy and magical intention. Take the salt out of your home and dispose of it at least a block away. Your stone is now ready to serve your needs.

gratitude for gifts from nature

Stones, crystals, and gems are regarded as the purest forms of the earth's generosity. Whenever you get a new crystal or a piece of jewelry with a stone or gem or decorate your home or garden with rocks and pebbles, show gratitude for these gifts from nature. This spell combines the power of crystals and that of thankfulness.

GATHER TOGETHER

small handful of daisies

small cup of thyme

small cup of ground cinnamon

stick of cinnamon incense

matches

Sprinkle the daisy blossoms, thyme, and ground cinnamon on your garden path and on your doorstep. Push the incense stick into the ground by the path and light it. Stand on the threshold of your door and chant aloud:

Mother Nature, I thank you for the strength

And bounty of your stones and bones.

Your beauty is reflected now and forever.

Blessed be all, Blessed be thee.

Leave the flowers, herbs, and spice on the path—every time you step on them, you are activating blessings. Your gratitude will be rewarded tenfold, and you will enjoy a shower of crystals and gems in your life from Mother Nature, who enjoys getting credit for her good works!

healing stones

ROSE QUARTZ

We all get worn down now and again. The wonderful thing is that crystals have the power to lift your mood, and there are a number of suggested stones on the following pages.

However, if you have no other crystal, make sure to have rose quartz on hand. Widely known as the stone of unconditional love, rose quartz is said to attract and inspire love in all forms. It's especially good for promoting self-love and emotional harmony. It can be a teeny tiny pebble of pink or a big ol' rock but you should have it near you, especially when you are feeling low. Keeping a piece of rose quartz out where you can see it—on your desk at work, on your nightstand, or next to the bathtub—can act as a powerful visual reminder to take a little bit of time for yourself.

revitalize with rosy stones

If you want to jump-start your life and bring about positive change, tap into the power of the rose and red stones. As well as rose quartz, other stones on this side of the color spectrum contain life's energy and can help you become more motivated, more energetic, and more vibrant, and also give you an appealing aura. Wear these rosy and red stones or keep them close by for an instant boost:

- Alexandrite
- Carnelian
- Garnet
- Red coral
- Red jasper
- Rhyolite
- Rose jasper
- Ruby

crystal chakra healing

By working with both your chakras (see page 39) and certain crystals, you can become much more in touch with your body and soul. The box below provides just a few examples of how to apply stones directly to your body or that of anyone else who needs healing.

pairing crystals with the chakras

- **Azurite** on the brow opens the third eye and deepens wisdom; this can balance the energy of the head and allow more light into the third eye.
- **Lapis lazuli** and its fellow blue crystal aquamarine can be laid on the throat chakra to release any blockage there. This greatly aids self-expression and is wonderful for professional speakers, as well as performers, such as actors and singers.
- **Malachite**, a heart stone, placed near the heart and along the center of the abdomen will create a sense of harmony and help you to let go of pain, suffering, and childhood wounds.
- **Turquoise** laid on the face—cheeks, forehead, and chin—is a calming agent, significantly reducing tension.

MALACHITE

mineral medicine

Since the dawn of humankind, people have carried stones and crystals as helpers and as talismans; for protection and good luck. In so doing, they have brought themselves a greater sense of security. For peace of mind, the strongest "medicine" consists of an amethyst, a rhodochrosite, and a turquoise, which are commonly available in metaphysical stores.

GATHER TOGETHER

amethyst crystal

rhodochrosite crystal

turquoise crystal

small sky-blue bag

Place the crystals in the bag. When you are ready, hold the pouch in your hand and incant:

Stones of the earth,
Warmed by the sun,
Clear away trouble,
Help and healing is now begun.

I recommend leaving your pouch on your altar where it can be at the ready whenever needed.

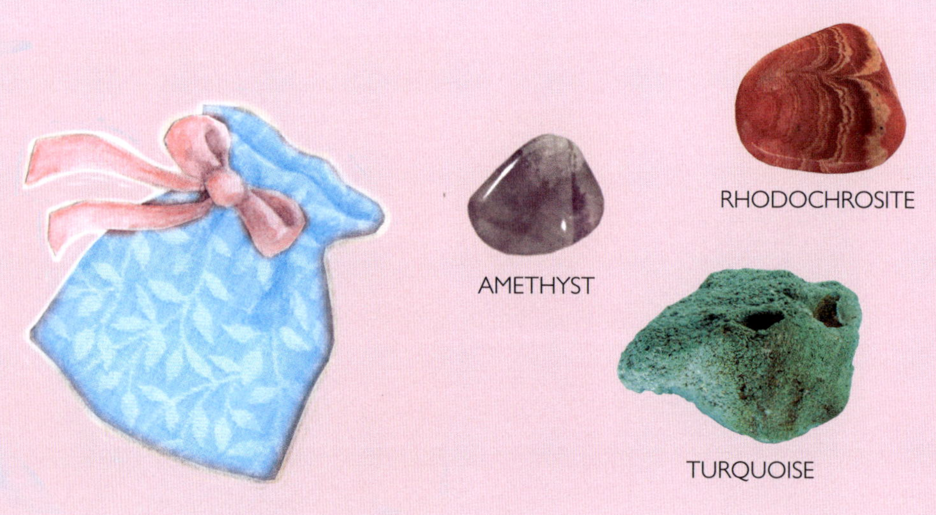

the healing power of jade

If you are hurting, hold a piece of jade of the color that suits your need best (see the box below) and say:

My heart is heavy and hurting,
I ask the universe for relief.
Harm to none but release for me,
I long to heal and be free,
And so it is.

GREEN JADE

colors of jade and their uses

- **Blue jade** is a rock for patience and composure and for conveying a sense of control. Wear blue jade pendants for serenity.
- **Green jade** is the counselor stone and can help a relationship that isn't working to become functional instead of dysfunctional. This shade is also a boon for the brain. Green jade helps with getting along.
- **Purple jade** heals a broken heart, allowing understanding and acceptance in, and pain and anger out. If you are going through a breakup, purple jade will help you with the heartache.
- **Red jade** promotes the proper release of anger and also generates sexual passion. Serve your lover a passion potion in a cup of carved red jade while wearing only red jade. Sparks will fly!
- **Yellow jade** is for energy, simple joy, and maintaining a sense of being a part of a greater whole. Yellow jade jewelry will help you to feel that all is well in your world.

centering earth stones

Crystals can have grounding, earthly qualities that you can harness to center your being to a place of calm and focus.

- Jasper: This stone has been valued for its healing and grounding energies since ancient times. Jasper carries strong earth energy, helping to deepen your personal connection with the earth when you wear or meditate with it. I recommend either brown or red jasper, both of which are healing stones that also give you great strength and heighten energy.
- K2: This crystal has recently become more popular, but it will be a new discovery for many people. K2 is a combination of grounding granite and celestial azurite, which balances our earthbound life experiences with our higher consciousness and connection to the universe and the heavens. It helps you connect to your intuition and find the balance between your intuition and your daily life. If you are wrestling with a real issue in your life or need to make a difficult choice where the options are unclear, call upon K2 and use it in meditation. Soon, the answers will come.
- Moss agate: This is a quartz that has a plantlike pattern caused by metallic crystalline grains. It is a power stone associated with the metal-rich planet Mercury and all things related to the mind. It makes a great grounding stone for those who can get too caught up in their thoughts and those who need help keeping their feet on the ground. If you ever find your mind racing or worried thoughts creeping in, get your hands on a moss agate and you'll feel the reassurance of this rock.
- Smoky quartz: Another beautifully grounding and stabilizing crystal, smoky quartz has the effect of making you feel deeply rooted to the earth. It is very centering in an uplifting way and it works to counteract any negative vibrations, replacing them with the positive.

rock steady: a grounding ritual

Simplicity is the key to the effectiveness of this rite. All you need is a brown candle and an earth stone. My preference is moss agate—I keep a piece of it on my work shrine and if times are especially intense or worrisome, I carry it with me.

GATHER TOGETHER

brown candle

matches

earth stone (see opposite)

Take the candle and crystal and place them both on the floor. Light the candle and sit in front of it with your stone in your hand. Touch your stone to your forehead and say aloud:

Worry and fear,
Are no longer here.
This is my touchstone, strong and true,
Come what may, I have the power to renew.
With harm to none and blessings to all,
So mote it be.

Now close your eyes and hold the stone in both your hands. Notice how a feeling of grounding rises up through your body to the top of your head.

MOSS AGATE

the pagan path: walking meditation with a crystal

For centuries, in group rituals and solo spells, witches have walked specific paths in the form of symbolic shapes that hold potent spiritual meaning. These prayer walks represent a journey to our own center and back again out into the world—this is some of the inner work we witches need to do now and again. All you need for this ritual is a stone that brings you special inspiration. Prepare for this walking meditation when the moon is in Sagittarius, Aquarius, or your natal moon sign. (If you don't know your moon sign, consult an astrologer or the recommended astrology resources on page 140.)

First, you should plan your path. You may find one walking pattern to be especially enriching for you. I recommend walking the figure eight—the "eternity" symbol. Otherwise, choose from among the universal shapes in the box opposite. I suggest always walking sunwise, or clockwise. You can walk a distance of your choice—a small distance in your living room, a bigger shape in your backyard, or whatever feels right to you, intuitionally. For the more complicated patterns, you can draw them on paper and place it where you can see it to use as a guide.

universal shapes

- **Circle:** The shape of the sun and moon. It designates the whole, the complete, that which never ends and encompasses all.
- **Cross:** The form of a human figure with arms outstretched from the center. The importance of this symbol predated Christianity by millennia.
- **Five-pointed star:** This resembles the human form with arms and legs outspread—Leonardo Da Vinci's favorite.
- **Hexagram:** In the Jewish tradition, the beloved. It is two triangles intersecting, the meeting of heaven and earth.
- **Oval:** The shape that designates the spirit and divine being.

Once you have chosen the right path for you, consider which stone will be best to carry with you. Maybe it is your birthstone; perhaps it is a jade talisman, a calming quartz, an intuition-boosting amethyst or labradorite. Choose your stone and place it in your pocket. You are now ready to begin your walk. Keep your eyes closed for the first step, then open your eyes and pray aloud as you walk:

Guide my steps; help me to walk in wisdom.
What I seek on this day, I shall find as I go,
With an open heart and mind.
Today, I receive the blessings of the sun.

QUARTZ

elixir of enchantment

Adding a tiny crystal to potions harnesses the energy of the crystal. For example, amethyst is a calming crystal that will add serenity to your space in a home mister.

GATHER TOGETHER

1-fluid ounce (30-ml) blue spray bottle

distilled water

small amethyst crystal

neroli essential oil

vanilla essential oil

Fill the bottle three-quarters full with the distilled water. Drop in the tiny crystal so it floats down to the bottom of the bottle. Add 3 drops each of the neroli and vanilla essential oils and seal the bottle. Shake it gently. Before spraying around your home, chant aloud:

This is a home of peace.

This is a home of happiness.

Happiness lives here.

Healthiness lives here.

And so it is.

AMETHYST

stone of self-belief

Hematite shores up self-image and self-belief. It also transforms negative energy into positive. Hematite is considered to be yang, a more male energy. My preferred aspect of this shiny wonder is that it assists with both legal problems and astral projection. Hematite is a creativity crystal and a marvelous mental enhancer, increasing the ability to think with logic, to focus, to concentrate, and to remember more clearly and completely. Hematite draws anxiety out of the body and creates calm.

In addition to all of these outward-projecting aspects, hematite contributes to inner work: self-knowledge, deeper consciousness, and wisdom. Like the iron in the earth from which it is formed, hematite grounds. If you feel spacey or disconnected, you should wear hematite. Hematite contains tremendous grounding energy that makes you feel like you are literally one with the earth.

Touch it to your skin and feel the magnetic energy. It is this effect that will make you feel more balanced, calm, and centered. Hematite stones also soak up any negative energy within your body or energy field. After you have used it, you should place the stone in a bowl of pure salt to cleanse it.

HEMATITE

scrying stones

The great seers can use a mirror, a still surface of water, or any reflective surface for prophetic purpose. Any polished stone can serve the same purpose.

Sit in a darkened room, hold the smooth stone in your hand, and gaze at it. It may take a few moments but you will begin to see flickering and even images on the surface. What you see are messages specifically for you. I suggest you keep a scrying record in your Book of Shadows (see page 27). Here are some marvelous crystals you can use for divination:

- **Amethyst** opens your psychic abilities.
- **Azurite with malachite** can help you to conceive new ideas.
- **Bloodstone** guards you against deceit from others.
- **Celestite** gives you the very special help of angel-powered insight and advice.
- **Chrysocolla** helps you to foresee difficulties, including romantic ones.
- **Lapis lazuli** leads the way for the new in your life.
- **Selenite** can be used under moonlight for visions of your ideal future.

AMETHYST

AZURITE WITH MALACHITE

BLOODSTONE

CELESTITE

moonstone runes

MOONSTONE

Moonstone is reputed to be the most powerful crystal for use in rune stones—the tools used for a specialized form of divination. Runes are letters from a language used by early Nordic peoples, which are carved into the stones and said to hone and intensify the intuition of the reader divining the future from them.

You, too, can use a bag of lustrous and mysterious small moonstones to get in touch with your powers of perception. While others may read their horoscopes with their morning coffee, you can take out a moonstone, look at the pattern carved in its beautifully reflective surface, and contemplate its meaning for your day.

CHRYSOCOLLA

LAPIS LAZULI

SELENITE

CHAPTER FIVE

moon magic: lunar energy for well-being and joy

Do you gaze up at the night sky in wonder? I know I do, nearly every night. The moon is both magical and majestic, mysterious and reflective. Let Luna be your guide as you design and develop your own moon ceremonies and rites of the night.

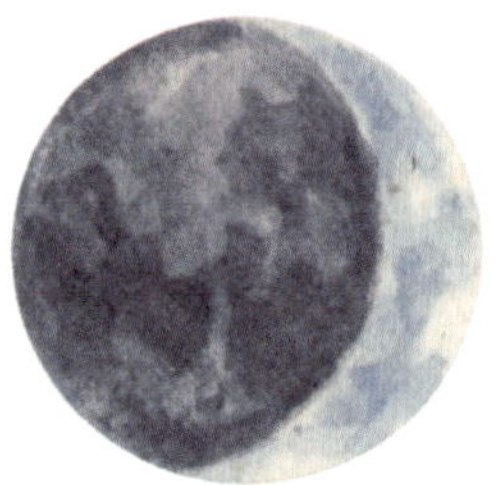

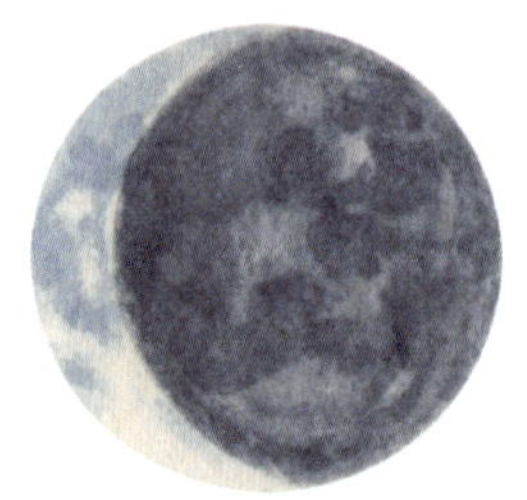

the phases of the moon

The proper phase of the moon is essential for spellcraft. Each lunar cycle begins with a new moon phase. This takes place when the moon lies between the sun and the Earth so the moon's illuminated side cannot be seen from the Earth. The moon gradually waxes (grows), moving to the opposite side of the Earth and, when it has reached the far side, its illuminated side faces us as the full moon. As it completes its orbit around the planet, it wanes until it apparently vanishes, reaching the new moon phase again. The entire cycle, during which the moon orbits the earth, takes approximately a month.

Each moon phase has a distinct energy that is conducive to certain spells, and we'll explore this in more detail over the following pages. Matching your magical intention to the moon phase is a really smart move.

the triple goddess

The Triple Goddess has three aspects: the maiden, a young, sweet girl; the mother, who births us all; and the crone, the wise older woman. The three faces of the Triple Goddess are reflected by the waxing, full, and waning phases of the moon.

timing your rituals with astrology

Incorporating your own astrological chart will help refine your spellwork enormously. The moon moves into a new sign every two to three days, and knowing when the moon aligns with your sign is essential. To determine the sun sign governing the moon on any given day, you will need a celestial guide or almanac (there are wonderful options online, such as www.cafeastrology.com—see page 140 for more details).

Through this enjoyable and inspiring process, I know that the moon in Scorpio is a powerful time for me to perform rites about love and romance, and that the moon in Pisces is also a fruitful time. Your magic is singular to you. By paying attention to the movements of the moon and stars in the sky, you can customize your craft to what works best for you.

In addition to the personal power of your own sun sign, there are multitudinous associations with the moon that can work in your favor, from colors and crystals to deities and days of the week. The more corresponding energies you can weave into your spellwork, the better the outcome. See the correspondence charts on the following pages to align your magical intentions.

new moon

Also known as the dark moon, the new moon is the beginning of the cycle and is an excellent time to start new endeavors and bring new energy into your life. "Budding" and "building" are the key words for the new moon.

This phase is a wonderful opportunity to involve yourself in personal improvement and transformation, whether spiritual or health-related, from practicing yoga to following a new diet. I also try to start new ventures during this phase. It's the perfect time to plant a garden, reorganize an office, start a new business, begin an art project, or embark on a new relationship—anything that requires energy for developing and growing. The new moon also has great advantages for healing. Rituals and charms commenced in the new moon tend to have tangible results by the next new moon.

correspondences for new beginnings

- **Days:** Monday and Sunday.
- **Colors:** Black, dark blue, and deep purple.
- **Herbs:** Agrimony, chamomile, lavender, mugwort, passionflower, and yarrow.
- **Incense:** Basil, cinnamon, ginger, lavender, myrrh, and rose.
- **Essential oils:** Lavender and roman chamomile.
- **Crystals:** Black tourmaline, labradorite, lapis lazuli, obsidian, and smoky quartz.
- **Metal:** Silver.

diana's bow

The new moon is sometimes called Diana's Bow, a reference to the Roman goddess of the hunt. This maiden phase (see the box on page 102) arrives when the moon begins to show its first glimmering crescent of light, reminiscent of the goddess's favored weapon. You can call upon Diana during your magical workings and ask her to bestow favor on your new projects.

incantation for new ideas

The first night of the new moon is the best time to sow the seeds for the things you want to bring into your life and your future. Fresh ideas, innovation, and inspiration will be yours with this dark moon magic.

GATHER TOGETHER

purple cloth

3 purple candles

smudging bundle of dried lavender blooms

fireproof dish

matches

lavender essential oil

Pick a spot outside—your backyard, deck, or somewhere outside your home is perfect for this rite. Lay the purple cloth on the ground and set the purple candles on this "mobile altar." Set down the smudging bundle in a fireproof dish and light with the matches.

Using the matches, scratch your name into the first candle. Scratch your hope into the second candle (with as much brevity as possible—"new ideas" or "artistic vision" will work well, as long as it is true to your intention). On the third candle, inscribe a circle representing the energy of the dark moon. Anoint the three candles with the lavender essential oil.

Light your name candle with a match and recite:

This candle burns for me.

Light the candle of hope and say:

Here burns my hope for [your intention].

Light the third candle—the candle of inspiration—and say:

Here burns the flame of my mind, alight and alive with new ideas.

With your eyes closed, picture yourself enacting your hope and desire. Picture yourself in the company of a person who inspires you and imagine them walking beside you, encouraging you to achieve your goal. After a few minutes, extinguish the candles and smudging bundle in the fireproof dish.

Place all the ritual elements on your main altar inside your home for the remaining days of the dark moon phase. Get ready for an abundance of inspiration and inventive ideas to come your way.

waxing moon

While waxing, the moon grows steadily larger and so this phase is best for matters of abundance, completing goals, and building toward an outcome. Ceremonies for luck, growth, and love will succeed during the waxing moon.

love and romance

The moon is in full maiden aspect (see the box on page 102) for the fourteen days of the typical waxing period. The waxing moon is a time for relationships to flourish. If you are fortunate enough to have a soulmate, or if there is someone you would like to get to know better, the waxing moon is the perfect phase to seal your fate together. Power up this lunar influence with other correspondences (see right) to ensure that you are lucky in love. Friday, for example, is associated with Venus and its ruling goddess of love.

correspondences for love

- **Day:** Friday.
- **Colors:** Pink and red.
- **Herbs:** Aster, beet, bleeding heart, cardamom, chestnut, chickweed, elm, lovage, pear, pimento, plumeria, and rose.
- **Incense:** Amber, gardenia, hibiscus, jasmine, orange, rose, and strawberry.
- **Essential oils:** Carnation, dragon's blood, ginger, jasmine, myrtle, rose, and ylang-ylang.
- **Crystals:** Blue topaz, chryscholla, garnet, jade, rhodochrosite, rose quartz, serpentine, and tourmaline.
- **Metal:** Nickel.

prosperity and plenty

The waxing moon phase is a fortuitous time for manifesting magic and, as the moon burgeons during this phase, tap into its power to bring forth abundance and prosperity.

Thursdays are considered a day of luck and plenty and, along with other magical correspondences (see right), you can incorporate Thursday's divine influence into your money magic for that extra heavenly boost. Thursdays are named for the powerful Norse god, Thor, and I often refer to this day as "Thor's day." Thursdays are also ruled by Jupiter, who stands for joviality, expansion, and all things abundant. I was born on a Thursday, too, which makes me feel like it is even more of a day of good fortune for me.

correspondences for abundance

- **Day:** Thursday.
- **Color:** Green.
- **Herbs:** Almond, bergamot, ginger, golden seal, grapes, moonwort, moss, nasturtium, oakmoss, and sarsaparilla.
- **Incense:** Basil, bergamot, jasmine, oakmoss, orange, patchouli, and vetiver.
- **Essential oils:** Bergamot, cinnamon, eucalyptus, lemongrass, and sandalwood.
- **Crystals:** Aventurine, blue topaz, jade, and serpentine.
- **Metals:** Copper and silver.

SERPENTINE

full moon

When the moon is full, Mother Moon is at her zenith, parading in all her glory across the night sky. The full moon is pure power—her luminous glow surrounds us and promotes strength and supremacy. Rituals during this phase can be transformative, calling forth your personal power.

Take time, also, to honor lunar deities during this phase. The best way to acknowledge their influence and importance in our lives is to honor them outside, under a moonlit night sky. Always speak the names of lunar goddesses aloud in gratitude. Using candles or a bonfire during these magical workings will reflect and enhance the light of our lunar queens of the night.

The full moon also enhances psychic awareness, so cleanse your scrying mirrors, tarot decks, and crystals. Prophecy and divinatory rituals performed during this time can bring great clarity.

correspondences for creativity

- **Days:** Sunday and Wednesday.
- **Colors:** Orange and yellow.
- **Herbs:** Angelica, basil, coltsfoot, crocus, hemp, kava kava, and rosemary.
- **Incense:** Cinnamon and peppermint.
- **Essential oils:** Cinnamon, lavender, and rosemary.
- **Crystals:** Agate, aventurine, blue lace agate, carnelian, kunzite, lapis lazuli, opal, and topaz.
- **Metals:** Copper and gold.

once in a blue moon

The phrase "once in a blue moon" refers to rare and special occasions. How do we know when the blue moon occurs? It is on that remarkable instance when two full moons occur in one calendar month to give us an "extra," or thirteenth, full moon of the year.

Every witch is a soulful person and the blue moon is an occasion for deep spellcasting for these true spiritual seekers. Try the Blue Moon Spiritual Heights Spell (see pages 112–113) to tap into the transformational magic of this special celestial moment and reach your full spiritual potential.

The blue moon is to be used wisely. Take this opportunity to consider long-term plans and goals and to give thanks for what you have accomplished. As you take stock, be grateful for what you have and for the people in your life—good health, children, a job you enjoy, good friends, a comfortable home, and all the opportunities before you. All blue moon rituals should contain an aspect of thanksgiving, to the gods and goddesses and to Mother Nature, who gave you life.

blue moon spiritual heights spell

Many pagans believe the full moon to be the phase with the most potent power. If so, the rare, second full moon in a month will have the most extraordinary strength of all. Perform this spell outside at twilight on the first night of the blue moon to bring new understanding into your life and, perhaps, even an epiphany or two.

GATHER TOGETHER

yellow scarf or cloth

outdoor altar, small table, or three-legged stool

large yellow candle

rosemary essential oil

2 copper pennies

round, blue dish

matches

cinnamon incense

fireproof dish

yellow sheet (like a bedsheet or other material)

paper and pen

Place the yellow cloth over your outdoor altar. Anoint the yellow candle with the rosemary essential oil and place it in the middle of the altar. Place the two copper pennies (which represent both the full moons of this month) in the dish and place the dish in front of the candle. Light the candle with the matches and then light the cinnamon incense from the candle and place in the fireproof dish. Unfold the yellow sheet and spread it in front of the altar. Lay down on the sheet where you can see the bright, beautiful blue moon above you. Speak aloud the words opposite.

Sister Moon who shines so bright

Tonight, I take shelter under your light.

I feel love and healing from you this night.

Please shower upon me your wisdom
and insight.

Please teach me all that is good and right.

I thank you for these mysteries I will write.

Blessed be thee; so mote it be.

Gaze at the moon above and take in its rare glory. As you appreciate your surroundings and reflect on your blessings, relax and enjoy the respite. Allow insights to flow down to you. As new ideas and inspiration begin to flow—and they will—note them down. Take your time and don't rush as this may block the blessings.

When you are ready, rise, and extinguish the candle and incense. Pack up the ritual elements but leave the two pennies outside, tucked away in a place where they are "hidden in plain sight," and can absorb and reflect the light of every full moon. Make sure you look back and reflect on your notes at every full moon. New insight and understanding will continue to come, long after this ritual has been completed.

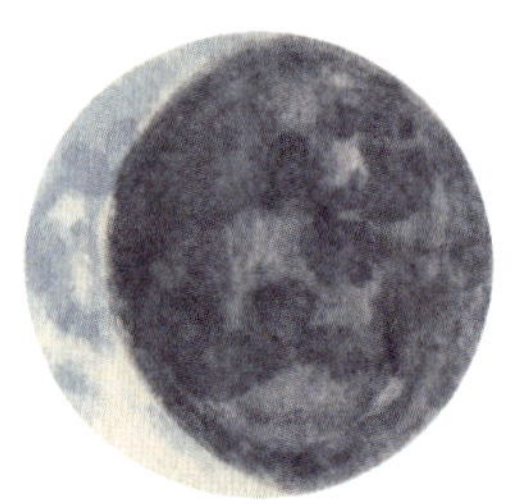

waning moon

The moon has reached her zenith and now begins her journey home, completing her orbit around the Earth. As she returns, her energy ebbs and she begins to wane and grow smaller. This phase, for us too, is a time to wind down any personal challenges and see them to an end. Conserve your power and turn your attention toward home and inner peace and wisdom.

finding peace

A peaceful life is a happy life. A state of peacefulness in your own heart can help instill more of that hopeful and positive energy into the world. Take care to rest and replenish during this waning moon phase.

correspondences for peace

- **Day:** Monday.
- **Colors:** Blue, pink, and white.
- **Herbs:** Chamomile, gardenia, lavender, lily of the valley, myrtle, passionflower, tuberose, vervain, and violet.
- **Incense:** Chamomile, gardenia, lavender, lilac, and sandalwood.
- **Essential oils:** Chamomile, gardenia, lavender, sandalwood, and violet.
- **Crystals:** Celestite, chryscholla, kunzite, lepidolite, pink quartz, rhodochrosite, and selenite.
- **Metal:** Copper.

creating a sanctuary

Spellcasting during the waning moon phase should also be concerned with conserving energy, creating a peaceful sanctuary full of positivity, so you can rest and replenish. The home is a sanctuary, a sacred space that protects you and your loved ones. Anyone, especially the highly sensitive or psychic, will pick up on lingering vibrations, so it is important to keep your space fresh, healthy, and free of negative energies and chemicals. Whether you are moving into a new home, have frequent visitors, or simply need to rest and replenish, it is of vital importance to clear out old, stale, and possibly negative energies from your domain.

correspondences for protection

- **Days:** Tuesday, Wednesday, Thursday, Friday, and Saturday.
- **Colors:** Black, blue, purple, red, and white.
- **Herbs:** Anise, bay laurel, blueberry, chives, chrysanthemum, dogwood, lemon, rose, and snapdragon.
- **Incense:** Anise star, clove, grapefruit, lavender, pine, and willow.
- **Essential oils:** Amber, angelica, carnation, cedarwood, eucalyptus, hyacinth, and rose geranium.
- **Crystals:** Black jasper, blue lace agate, desert rose, goldstone, red jasper, and tanzanite.
- **Metals:** Bronze, iron, lead, steel, and titanium.

CHAPTER SIX

the wheel of the year: festivals and celebrations

The pagan Wheel of the Year turns on the holidays, each one a seasonal highlight for pagans. They are a time to share sacred rites, good food and drink, and to revel in the joy of being in community. Nearly all our festivals have roots in the ancient rites based in fertility and the hopes of abundant farm crops.

the sabbats

The human heart longs for ritual and ways to mark life passages. The pagan calendar does that wonderfully by reminding us of the cycles of nature and the importance of spending time in community. Sabbats are the holy days for each

the four major sabbats

SAMHAIN (also known as Hallows, All Hallow's Eve, and Halloween)
Date: October 31
Colors: Purple, deep red, brown, and deep orange.
Altar offerings: Carved pumpkins, orange leaves, sweet pumpkin or chocolate spirit cakes, and a goblet of red wine.
Intention: *As the veil between worlds disappears this day, I call upon the elders, ancestors, and loved ones who have crossed over for wisdom.*

IMBOLC (also known as Candlemas and Saint Brigid's Day)
Date: February 2
Colors: White, light blue, and light green.
Altar offerings: Sprouting seeds, a goblet of cider, and first blossoms, such as snowdrops and crocuses.
Intention: *As the season begins to shift from winter, so will I open to inner change.*

BELTANE
Date: April 30/May 1
Colors: Grass green and pink.
Altar offerings: Spring leaves, a bowl of newly fallen rain, brightly colored ribbons, small herbs, and mayflowers.
Intention: *I celebrate the warmth of spring and the fire of love in my life.*

LAMMAS (also known as Lughnasadh and Lúnasa)
Date: August 2
Colors: Bright green and gold.
Altar offerings: Berries, vegetables from the garden, leaves, brightly colored flowers in full bloom, and a loaf of bread.
Intention: *As harvest season begins, I am grateful for and will share this bounty of blessings.*

season of the year. There are four major sabbats and four lesser sabbats, with the lesser sabbats being the astrological markers of new seasons. The Samhain festival on October 31 marks the beginning of the pagan year. Mark your witchy calender with these sabbats as they will become anchoring events in your year—and life. In this chapter, we will explore each sabbat in turn.

the four lesser sabbats

YULE (the winter solstice)
Date: December 21
Colors: White, light blue, silver, and black.
Altar offerings: A bowl of snow, winter photos, seeds, and icicle-shaped clear crystals.
Intention: *I intend to spend this shortest day in community with friends, family, and fellow pagans to share our stories and strengthen connections.*

OSTARA (the vernal or spring equinox)
Date: March 21
Colors: Light green and light yellow.
Altar offerings: Seedlings, budding and sprouting branches, a bowl of flower bulbs, and eggs.
Intention: *On this day when light is in balance, I fully embrace sacred self-care for balance and in my life and work.*

LITHA (the summer solstice)
Date: June 21
Color: Bright yellow.
Altar offerings: Freshly foraged weeds and herbs, veggies, leaves, and fruit.
Intention: *On this midsummer day with the sun's full power, I own my full personal power to bring dreams into fruition.*

MABON (the autumnal equinox)
Date: September 22
Colors: Gold, brown, and orange.
Altar offerings: Squash and pumpkins, bounty from the garden, acorns and other nuts, colored leaves, corn, and fall flowers.
Intention: *As summer shifts to fall, I will let go of anything which no longer serves me.*

samhain

Celebrated on October 31, Samhain (also known as Halloween, among other names) stems from the grand tradition of the Celtic New Year. What started as a folk festival celebrated by small groups in rural areas has come to be the second largest holiday nowadays in North America and is increasingly gaining popularity in the UK and the rest of Europe. There are multitudinous reasons, including modern marketing, but I think it satisfies a basic human need to let your "wild side" out, to be free and more connected with the ancient ways.

honoring the ancestors

This is the time when the veil between worlds is thinnest and you can commune with the other side, with elders, and the spirit world. It is important to honor the ancestors during this major sabbat and acknowledge what transpired in the passing year as well as set intentions for the coming one. Invite your circle to take part in this ritual; the ideal number for your "coven" is 13.

GATHER TOGETHER

outdoor stone altar

powdered incense

three candles to represent the Triple Goddess (see page 102)

matches

salt

loaf of bread

goblets of wine

Let go of old sorrows, angers, and anything not befitting new beginnings in this new year. Bring only your best to this auspicious occasion. Pour the powdered incense onto the altar in a pentagram star shape.

Light the candles and say:

In honor of the Triple Goddess on this sacred night of Samhain,
All the ancient ones,
From time before time,
To those behind the veil.

Rap the altar three times and light the incense. Say this blessing aloud:

For this bread, wine, and salt,
We ask the blessings of Mother, Maiden, and Crone,
And the gods who guard the Gate of the World.

Sprinkle salt over the bread, eat the bread, and drink the wine. Each of the celebrants should come to the altar repeating the bread and wine blessing. After this, be seated and everyone in turn should name those on the other side and offer thanks to the ancestors and deities.

yule

Yule celebrates the winter solstice on December 21, traditionally in the northern hemisphere with rituals to welcome the rebirth of the sun. Pagans are community-oriented by nature and long ago, in northern climes, this seasonal festival was based on how best to get through—and, in some cases, survive—times of cold and scarcity by sharing food, supplies, and the nightly fire. These evening gatherings naturally led to much storytelling—many oral cultural traditions were born of fire.

winter solstice ritual

If the weather is mild, you can perform this rite outside, but if it is very cold, choose a room or space with a fireplace to ensure that this community celebration stays both comfortable and comforting as you gather to share your wishes for the warmer days to come.

GATHER TOGETHER

table to serve as an altar

white cloth

large bundle of evergreen

powdered incense

white votive candles (one for each attendee)

mugs (one for each attendee)

large thermos of celebratory drink (such as Bright Blessings Brew, see page 137)

firewood

aromatic kindling (such as applewood, birch, cedar, cherry, oak, palo santo, pear, pine, or pinion)

matches

ribbons

Cover the table with the white cloth and decorate with evergreen. Place the incense, candles, and mugs on the table along with the thermos. Once everyone is comfortably gathered, welcome folks and take a moment to acknowledge the background of this rite.

Build and light a fire with the wood, kindling, and matches, and light the candles and incense while the fire begins to build.

Using a couple of strands of the evergreens from the altar, fashion the branches into a crown, and secure with ribbon. Invite each participant to do the same. When everyone is wearing their crowns, form a semicircle around the fire. Now, say aloud:

As the sun returns, back to the earth, we gather here for shared joy and mirth, we commemorate life and death and rebirth.

Cold winter nights, frozen days so bright, a time of magic, at this longest night, without the dark, there cannot be light.

Thank you for the sun that gives us life, without beginning and without end, with gratitude on this solstice night, so mote it be! Blessed be!

Now, ask those gathered to serve themselves a drink, and to share their hopes and wishes for the coming spring. When the sharing winds down, close the ritual with a toast to the winter solstice.

Blessed be to the Mother Goddess and Father God.

We live in your light, everlasting in Eternity.

This ritual is now done!

As you pack up the mugs and other ritual elements, send the participants home with their herbal crowns and a candle each, as a memento of this sacred occasion and collective experience.

imbolc

Also known as Candlemas, Imbolc is a celebration of rebirth and renewal, held on February 2. In the northern hemisphere, it is a harbinger of spring, the midpoint between the winter solstice and the spring equinox.

Imbolc is also referred to as Saint Brigid's Day. It is said that Saint Brigid is a Christianization of the Celtic goddess, Brid, who was famous for her poetry, wisdom, and her care for others. In honor of Brid's protective qualities, Saint Brigid's day is a wonderful opportunity to honor new witches in your circle, and many Wiccans use the Imbolc sabbat to initiate new witches and acknowledge their progress on the path.

brigid's bowl: creamy potato soup

Perfect for an Imbolc celebration or initiation ceremony, this seasonal soup will warm body, heart, and soul.

GATHER TOGETHER

large saucepan

4 cups (900 ml) chicken stock

4 cups (900 ml) milk

8 tablespoons butter

large pot

1 cup (140 g) flour

6 bay leaves

½ teaspoon freshly ground black pepper

4 large baking potatoes, peeled and finely diced

1 teaspoon salt

6–8 small ovenproof bowls

sour cream, to serve

shredded Cheddar cheese, to serve

green (spring) onions, to serve

baking sheet

crispy bacon, to garnish (if desired)

spoons, for serving

Makes 6–8 cups of soup

In the saucepan, gently warm the chicken stock and milk over a medium-high heat.

Melt the butter in the separate pot. Add the flour, stirring constantly, to form a roux. Slowly add the stock and milk mixture, stirring vigorously to combine. Add the bay leaves, black pepper, potatoes, and salt. Simmer over a low heat for 15–20 minutes.

When the potatoes are tender and the soup has thickened, stir, lightly mashing the potatoes in the soup. Pour the soup into the bowls and top with sour cream, Cheddar cheese, and green (spring) onions.

Heat the broiler (grill) to low. Put the bowls on a baking sheet and broil for 1–2 minutes, until golden and bubbling. Garnish with crispy bacon (if using), and serve with the spoons.

This soup is a wonderful way to pay tribute to the hedge witches, hunters, gatherers, and gardeners who came before us and ensured the survival of their neighbors through hard work, practicality, and strong, generous hearts. Enjoy the merriment, the feasting, and the friendship.

ostara

Ostara celebrates the vernal or spring equinox on March 21, as the sun warms the northern hemisphere and spring approaches.

Ostara, or Eostre, the Saxon goddess, is the personification of the rising sun and is associated with the coming spring and radiant dawn. In some languages, her namesake is also known as the festival of Easter and legend has it that her totem—the rabbit—brought forth the brightly colored eggs now associated with this festival.

sweetest spring smoke clearing

To power up the equinox enchantment opposite, smudge the room with powerful herbal scents. Braided sheaves of sweetgrass, for example, have been burned in rituals for centuries to call forth ancestors and send away unwanted energy. See also pages 34–36.

spring equinox divination

Invite your guests to this simple and humble ritual, which befits the purity of the equinox. This spell invokes the full moon's divinatory powers (see page 110) to bring fresh inspiration and intentions for the seasons ahead. The four white candles represent each of the seasons, while the round, white bowl represents the full moon.

GATHER TOGETHER

small table, for an altar

4 white candles

matches

white spring flowers (such as crocus, lily, or snowdrop)

round, white bowl of freshly drawn water

bay laurel leaves, one for each attendee, in a basket

Invite all the attendees to take a seat in a circle around the altar. Light the candles with the matches. Scatter the white flowers in the bowl of water.

Pass the bowl and the basket of leaves around the circle. Invite each ritualist, one by one, to dip a leaf into the bowl of water, then touch the wet leaf to the third eye (located on

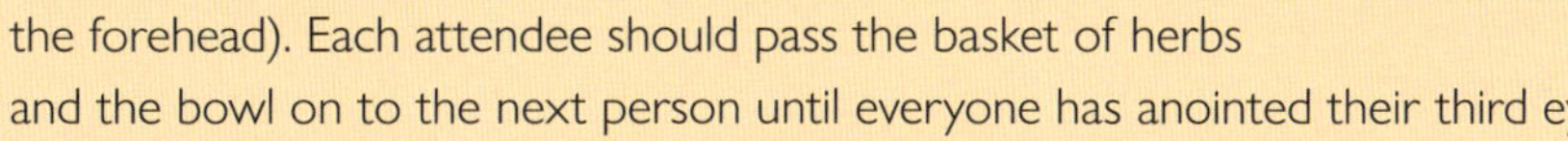

the forehead). Each attendee should pass the basket of herbs and the bowl on to the next person until everyone has anointed their third eye.

Now, each ritualist should clap resoundingly and say in turn:

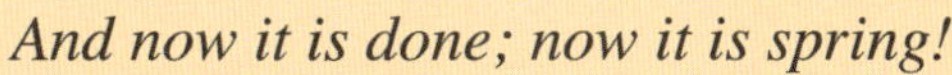

And now it is done; now it is spring!
It is spring in the East,
It is spring in the South,
It is spring in the West,
And it is spring in the North!
Blessed be we and thee!

Invite people to sit comfortably and share their insights and epiphanies, as the spirit moves them.

beltane

Witchy ones celebrate Beltane on the very last eve of April, and it is traditional for the festivities to go on all night. When the sun returns the following day—May Day—revelers erect a beribboned Maypole and dance around in most fanciful garb, a charming May Day tradition that continues after hundreds of years.

This is a holiday for feasting, laughter, and lots of flirty fun. Dancing is followed by pagan picnicking and relaxing togetherness. Celebrate this joyous seasonal event with a May Day picnic and bring plenty of mead, beer, wine, and cider.

may day picnic

Host a joyful spree to look forward to every May. Ask your guests to bring finger food and a colorful blanket for picnicking. Floral offerings to the gods and goddesses that provide us with such bounty and beauty should also be in plenitude. Try narcissus, daffodils, tulips, and freesias (my favorite) in bright, showy colors.

GATHER TOGETHER

large picnic table, for an outdoor altar

colorful, floral print tablecloth

compostable serveware (like napkins, cups, plates, and sporks)

multicolored ribbons, to represent the Maypole

floral incense (such as lavender, rosemary, jasmine, freesia, lilac, gardenia, or rose)

matches

fireproof dish

3 large cauldrons half-filled with water to serve as vases for the flowers

blankets and spreads for seating

Adorn the table with the cloth. Have your guests place their food and drinks on the altar alongside the serveware.

At the altar, offer the guests a ribbon or two to wear as headbands. As they tie the ribbons in their hair, they should speak aloud a wish for this new season of life. Each wish should come directly from the heart—it can be as simple as: "May this spring be bountiful so all may be fed."

Once everyone is adorned with ribbons and has spoken a personal intention, light the incense with the matches and place on the altar in a fireproof dish. As the spring smoke billows and perfumes the air, ask the guests to form a circle and sing the Beltane blessing:

Hoof and horn, hoof and horn,

Tonight our spirits are reborn,

Welcome joy into my home.

Fill my friends with love and laughter.

So mote it be.

Repeat the blessing twice. While everyone is still holding hands, ask each person around the circle in turn how they can bring more love into the world. Once done, repeat the blessing, and with the last "So mote it be," declare it to be feasting time. Be sure to drink in every drop of joy in this celebration—enough to last for the rest of the year! At the end of the ritual, ask participants to clean up, compost, and recycle to make sure your event is sacred and sustainable.

litha

In the northern hemisphere, the summer solstice takes place on June 21 and is truly a time to remember all the sheer abundance that our earth provides us. I have been heartened to see the increasing popularity of this joyous midsummer thanksgiving in recent years.

Let the season inspire you and gather information about the burgeoning herbs, flowers, and trees all around you. From our flourishing gardens to the bounty of our fields and forests, Litha is a wonderful season to witness the dual energy personified in Wicca tradition as the Lord and Lady of Magic (see opposite).

the lord and lady of magic

Wiccan tradition frequently addresses twin deities—dual energies that represent the twofold principles of feminine and masculine energy inherent in nature. This sacred connection to Earth and spirit can be traced far back in history to Paleolithic peoples, who worshipped a hunter god and a fertility goddess.

Wicca is enormously popular today, in part because it gives us freedom to create our own way of worshipping. By understanding the primal, dual aspect of nature, and seeing the world as revealed in these twin mysteries and myths, you can plan rituals that are customized to fit your truest nature.

the god

The God is represented by the sun. He is born on December 21 (the winter solstice) and grows steadily until June 21 (the summer solstice), when his power reaches its fullest. After midsummer (Litha), his power wanes and he expires with the shortening daylight hours. On the longest night of the year, he is reborn again. The energy of the God can be felt in the physical and tangible. He can be seen in the hunt, in the harvest, and in vitality, strength, sexuality, and passion.

the goddess

The Goddess is creator of all. This Great Mother is the keeper of the cycles of birth, life, death, and rebirth that are reflected in nature and the seasons. In some modern traditions, the God rules the physical world while the Goddess governs intuition, dreams, and the mind.

prayer to the lord and lady of magic

Ask your fellow pagan celebrants to bring an offering to this solstice gratitude ritual, to show thankfulness and appreciation for all received from these beneficent beings—flowers, fruit, a few words of gratitude, or perhaps even a verse of poetry.

GATHER TOGETHER

small stool or table, for an altar

green cloth

yellow and green crystals (peridot, jade, citrine, quartz, or similar)

yellow dish

representation of the god and goddess (such as a statue, painting, or an icon of a deity you have made)

2 candles (one green, one yellow)

matches

horn (or hollow tree branch), to represent the god

green bowl, to represent the goddess

wand

Set up your altar outside, ideally near a grove of trees that offers both sun and shade, and cover with the green cloth. Put the crystals in the yellow dish and place on the altar with the representations of the god and goddess. Light the candles with the matches and place the horn inside the green bowl.

Cast a magic circle with your wand by "casting" or drawing a boundary in the air (see page 41). Invoke the Lord and Lady by asking attendees to bring their offering to the altar as you chant aloud the words opposite.

Oh Lord and Lady, wise and true,
We will walk with thee in the path to the magical.
We thank you for all you have given, life itself.
We pledge ourselves to you, here and now,
On this sacred summer solstice day.
Thanks to you, inspiration we will never lack.
With gratitude for all the blessings, so mote it be.

As the candles burn, everyone gathered should remember the blessings they have received from the Lord and Lady of Magic through the years.

lammas

Lammas is celebrated on August 2 far and wide. The Celts called this time of the year Lughnasadh, or Lúnasa, for Lugh, a Celtic god of wisdom.

Lammas used to be known as "Lammastide," meaning "loaf time," and in the northern hemisphere is a celebration of the grain harvest when the grain can be baked into nourishing loaves of bread. The custom is that when the first grain of the season is cut, it must be baked into a loaf and offered to Lugh in a sort of thanksgiving devotion. This is a time of abundance—gather your friends together and be grateful for life's blessings.

lammas eve ritual

Show appreciation for the abundance of nature and the bounty of the harvest with your own unique celebration of the Lammas Day. It is a feast of singing, dancing, and storytelling that ends with gratitude and blessings. Don't forget to set a place for the great godly guest, Lugh.

GATHER TOGETHER

acorns

sheaves of grain

baskets of apples, pears, and oranges

cauldron

water (to three-quarter fill the cauldron)

essential oil (apple, lemon, orange, and pear work well)

votive candles (one for each attendee)

matches

floating candle

Create a sacred space by arranging the acorns, sheaves, and baskets of fruit to the north, south, east, and west of the cauldron. Fill the cauldron with the water and add the essential oil.

Light each of the votive candles with the matches, then hand them to each participant and form a circle around the cauldron. Next, the floating candle should be lit and placed in the cauldron. Speak the following:

Oh ancient Lugh of days long past,

Be here with us now,

In this place between worlds,

On this Lammas Day.

Rap three times on the cauldron. After a few moments, say:

Harvest is here and the seasons do change.

This is the height of the year.

The bounty of summer sustains us,

In spirit, in soul, and in body.

Now dance in procession, five times in a spiral around the cauldron. Singing and dancing is a part of this rite, and the procession can end with storytelling and expressions of gratitude for the gifts of the season and the riches of the harvest bounty.

The leader declares when the rite is finished by putting out the candles and proclaiming: "This rite is done."

mabon

The sabbat of Mabon represents the end of the fruit, vegetable, and grain harvest in northern climes. Gathering around a roaring bonfire with ale, wine, mead, and festival foods is the perfect celebration to give thanks for the harvested stores that will provide sustenance and ensure survival through the long, cold winters.

Traditionally celebrated at the autumn equinox on September 22, Mabon reminds us of the fact that winter is near and that community is not just about the bonds of family and friendship, but our very survival. Just as your Book of Shadows (see page 27) is a wonderful way to share knowledge with your coven, Mabon can keep the spirit of food-sharing alive in your community. I have an old apple tree that is fruitful, and I have made cider and simple apple sauce with the fruit, packing it in jars with colorful ribbons for my spiritual sisterhood. What can you make and share for the next Mabon observation?

The gift of food keeps cords of connection and community strong. Celebrate Mabon with family, friends, and neighbors, and remember—gatherings are much merrier with a hearty witch's brew (see opposite)! Pass the blessings on and they will return to you threefold.

bright blessings brew

This cup of comfort is brimming with a marvelous blend of herbs that not only have immune-boosting antioxidant properties but also help to brighten your mood and confer a sense of calm.

GATHER TOGETHER

3 cinnamon sticks

mixing bowl

1 teaspoon lemongrass

1 teaspoon fennel seeds

1 teaspoon grated lemon zest

2 tablespoons dried rose hips

wooden spoon

teapot

teakettle

tea strainer

mugs

honey (local, if possible)

Break the cinnamon sticks into pieces and put them into the bowl followed by all the herbs. Stir gently with the wooden spoon and place the herbal mixture into the teapot. Fill the kettle with water and, once boiled, pour into the teapot. Let the herbs steep for a half hour. Stir gently with the wooden spoon, strain, and pour into mugs. Add honey, to taste, and serve. To your health!

glossary

Aromatherapy: Fragrant essential oils extracted from plants applied through inhalation or topically on the skin used safely with intention for healing and to enhance rituals and spellwork.

Associations: The meanings attributed to various things such as herbs, colors, and crystals that help practitioners understand the significance of, use effectively in rituals, and personalize through experience.

Astral: Refers to connection with a non-physical realm where spiritual and mystical experiences occur in a space of personal exploration to seek guidance.

Clairvoyance: To have "clear seeing," i.e. the ability to see and perceive message that others cannot, including communication with the spirit world.

Cleansing: The process of clearing unwanted energy from an area, object, or person, often using the smoke from burning incense or sage smudge sticks.

Correspondences: A framework of specific symbolic links to select the right materials and tools for your spells ensuring they align with your intention.

Coven: A group of Wiccans who gather for rituals, shared experiences, and community support, enhancing spiritual growth.

Divination: Connecting with one's intuition to access deeper knowledge and guidance from the universe. Methods include rune stones, tarot cards, and crystal balls. See also *scrying*.

Elements: Refers to the four classical elements—earth, air, fire, and water—which hold particular energies that can be harnessed in ritual work.

Familiar: A special intuitive bond, typically with an animal spirit that acts as a companion and helper providing support, protection, and guidance during magical practices.

Gods and Goddesses: Central figures that symbolize the dualistic nature of divinity reflecting the interconnectedness of all life and the balance of feminine and masculine energies in the universe.

Intention: A clear and specific statement to focus on when performing spells or rituals serving as a guiding principle to help direct energy to manifest the desired outcome.

Sabbats: The eight seasonal Wiccan festivals forming the Wheel of the Year. They are deeply rooted in nature's rhythms to celebrate the cycles of life.

Scrying: A powerful divination practice of gazing into a reflective surface.

Smudging: The burning of sacred herbs, such as bundles of sage, to energetically clear a space in preparation for ritual.

Vibration: Refers to the emotional or energetic state or atmosphere of a person, place, or object.

Visualization: To imagine something in your mind's eye.

resources and further reading

crystals, herbs, oils, and other supplies

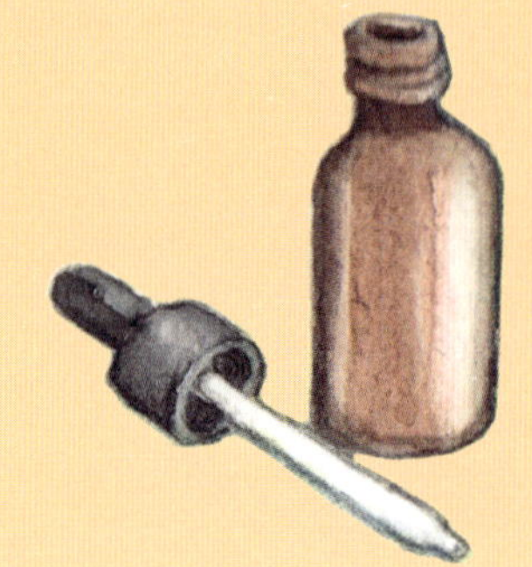

Crystal Age (www.crystalage.com)
For crystals, crystalline statuary, and jewelry.

Crystals by Nature (https://crystalsbynature.nl)
For crystals, gems, and jewelry.

Herbs & Arts (www.herbsandarts.com)
For herbs, oils, incense, burners, and candles.

astrology

Cafe Astrology (www.cafeastrology.com):
Hugely useful site for all your astrology needs.

To find out your sun sign:
www.cafeastrology.com/whats-my-sun-sign.html

To find out your moon sign:
www.cafeastrology.com/whats-my-moon-sign.html

books

If you liked this book, you might also like some of my others (all published by CICO Books):

The Green Witchery Tarot Deck (2026)
Wiccan Self-care Spells (2024)
Your Book of Shadows (2024)
Magic for Change (2023)
The Green Witch at Home (2022)
5-Minute Magic for Modern Wiccans (2022)
The Book of Witchy Wellbeing (2021)
The Book of Kitchen Witchery (2016)

And these ones by Silja (published by CICO Books):
The Green Wiccan Book of Herbs (2026)
Seasons of the Witch (2025)
Wicca for Everyday Life (2025)
The Green Wiccan Spell Book (2019)

index

acknowledgments

This book is one of the many blessings I am counting and it came about only because of the amazing talent, care, patience, and keen minds and eyes of this group of book goddesses: Emily Breen, Imogen Valler-Miles, Carmel Edmonds, and my very long-time friend and collaborator Kristine Pidkameny. My beautiful CICO books and I stand on the shoulders of these giant talents. Big gratitude! Blessed be!

picture credits

Illustrations by Emma Garner and crystal photography by Roy Palmer and Geoff Dann, all © CICO Books, except as listed below.

© Adobe Stock/anitapol: p. 34 (sweetgrass); © Adobe Stock/Arsenova: p. 35 (palo santo); © Adobe Stock/Elena: p. 47 (geode); © Adobe Stock/Julija: p. 59 (yin and yang); © Adobe Stock/Mariia: p. 41 (magic circle); © Adobe Stock/Polina: pp. 37, 38, 89 (chakras); © Adobe Stock/Tharindu: pp. 9, 29, 61, 81, 101, 117 (moon phases); © Adobe Stock/YAYORE: p. 26 (pendulum); © Julia Cellini: pp. 102, 104, 108, 110, 114 (moon phases)